Evangelism and Resistance in the Black Atlantic, 1760–1835

Evangelism and Resistance in the Black Atlantic, 1760–1835

CEDRICK MAY

The University of Georgia Press • Athens and London

© 2008 by the University of Georgia Press

Athens, Georgia 30602

All rights reserved

Set in Minion by Bookcomp, Inc.

Printed and bound by Maple-Vail

The paper in this book meets the guidelines for

permanence and durability of the Committee on

Production Guidelines for Book Longevity of the

Council on Library Resources.

Printed in the United States of America

12   11   10   09   08   C   5   4   3   2   1

Library of Congress Cataloging-in-Publication Data

May, Cedrick, 1969–

Evangelism and resistance in the Black Atlantic,

1760–1835 / Cedrick May.

    p. cm.

Includes bibliographical references and index.

ISBN-13: 978-0-8203-2798-3 (hardcover : alk. paper)

ISBN-10: 0-8203-2798-0 (hardcover : alk. paper)

1. American literature—African American authors—

History and criticism.   2. Christianity and

literature—United States—History—18th century.

3. Christianity and literature—United States—

History—19th century.   4. Religion and politics—

United States—History—18th century.   5. Religion

and politics—United States—History—19th century.

6. African Americans—Religion—History.

7. Civil rights—Religious aspects—Christianity.

8. African American evangelists.   I. Title.

PS153.N5M2695 2008

810.9'3823—dc22   2007039034

British Library Cataloging-in-Publication Data available

To my niece, Phylisa (1992–2000), the first Word of God I ever heard clearly

—Uncle Doo Dah

CONTENTS

ix Acknowledgments

1 Introduction

24 *Chapter One.* Jupiter Hammon and the Written Beginnings of Black Theology

49 *Chapter Two.* Phillis Wheatley and the Charge toward Progressive Black Theologies

64 *Chapter Three.* John Marrant and the Narrative Construction of an Early Black Methodist Evangelical

83 *Chapter Four.* Prince Hall and the Influence of Revolutionary Enlightenment Philosophy on the Institutionalization of Black Religion

98 *Chapter Five.* Richard Allen and the Further Institutionalization of Black Theologies

116 *Chapter Six.* Maria Stewart and the Mission of Black Women in Evangelicalism

127 Notes

143 Bibliography

153 Index

ACKNOWLEDGMENTS

I owe a debt of gratitude to many individuals and institutions for help, support, and input that have contributed to the completion of this book. First, I thank Carla Mulford, under whose supervision I began this project as a dissertation. I could not have asked for a better mentor and friend than Carla, who introduced me to the discipline of early American studies and encouraged me to pursue my interests. I thank the Gilder Lehrman Institute for American History for a summer 2002 fellowship in American civilization that allowed me to access the holdings of the New-York Historical Society Library. I would like to thank the *African American Review* for publishing an early version of my third chapter, as well as the review's readers for their valuable suggestions. I thank Penn State University for a university research grant as well as Auburn University for a humanities development grant and two competitive research grants. I also owe a debt to Auburn University's Office for Multicultural Affairs, which awarded me two Title VI Grants that allowed me time during the summer to focus on my research and finish my manuscript for publication. I also thank Phillip Lapsansky at the Library Company of Philadelphia for his assistance and suggestions while I was working in the Library Company's collections.

There are many colleagues, too numerous to name here, to whom I owe thanks. I single out Paula Backscheider and Hilary Wyss at Auburn University for their encouragement and aid. Paula in particular helped me to push forward with my project and gave me a wealth of advice on the process of preparing a scholarly book for publication.

I would also like to thank my junior high teacher and mentor, Mr. David Porter, who recognized my potential, taught me a love of books and reading, and focused my energies in the right direction when I was at a very formative age. Every young person should have as dedicated a teacher as him.

Finally, I thank my wife, Penelope Ingram, for her love and patience and for the vibrant conversations about race, theory, and ethics that aided me in thinking through some of the difficult theological ideas examined in this book.

INTRODUCTION

In 1778, five years after the slave Phillis Wheatley published *Poems on Various Subjects, Religious and Moral*, another writer, also a slave, sat down during a moment's respite to begin penning a response to the younger and more well-known poet's work. Now nearly sixty-seven, Jupiter Hammon, who had published a handful of poems in locally distributed broadsides, included his ideas on religion specifically as well as ideas that implied a certain political position. Wheatley, who was about nineteen in 1773, when she published her book, had accomplished the remarkable feat of producing a book that not only appealed to her readers' religious and moral sensibilities but also carried political weight, particularly on delicate matters of state such as the Stamp Act, the relationship of a king to his subjects, and issues relating to slavery. It was a bold pronouncement for any writer, especially for a young, African slave woman on the eve of the American Revolution.

When Hammon wrote to Wheatley in verse, he established a precedent in North American and African American literary history: while African Americans certainly may have written themselves into being and recorded history through their individual literary voices, their writings were more than personal; they collectively established blacks as part of a new tradition in which African Americans considered their positions and conditions in print media and attempted to establish a means by which to understand and involve themselves in the immediate social and cultural world around them.

Where the Conversations Begin

Unlike Wheatley, Hammon was reticent, if not downright hostile, to the idea of involving himself in secular matters such as the politics and ideals of the American Revolution. In fact, he despised the war and thought of the belligerents' efforts as anti-Christian:

> Believe me now my Christian friends,
> Believe your friend call'd Hammon:
> You cannot to your God attend,
> and serve the God of Mammon.[1]

The war was anathema to him: its existence flew against the principles of the Christianity he personally embraced. His Calvinist-influenced Christianity had been bestowed on him by his enslavers—a Christianity, taught particularly to slaves, that strictly divided earthly political and spiritual matters.[2] To Wheatley he advised,

> While thousands muse with earthly toys;
> and range about the street,
> Dear Phillis, seek for heaven's joys,
> where we do hope to meet.[3]

Unlike Puritan evangelical Calvinists of the era, who "emphasized participation in the world with a view toward transforming it,"[4] Hammon was a Calvinist who did not believe that Christians, and even less so slaves, should do anything that distracted from contemplation of a heavenly afterlife. He believed that concepts such as freedom and equality were for a time to come, in the Kingdom of Heaven, not for the present. His poetic response to Wheatley was an argument, albeit a friendly one, in his mind, and he banked that his seniority in years and experience would lend his message the gravity to influence the younger poet to take quieter and more accommodating positions concerning her religion and politics.

Wheatley, however, was of another generation and mind-set from Hammon. Four decades younger than Hammon and, unlike him, having endured the Middle Passage at age five or six, Wheatley nonetheless was fortunate enough to have acquired something of a formal classical education and was allowed to cultivate her intellectual talents through study and exposure to the theology and political ideals of the time and place in which she lived. As a result, she eventually embraced universal republicanism and through her poetry found a voice and a platform with which to argue on behalf of herself and other Africans who endured the "tyrannic sway" of the "Modern Egyptians" who practiced slavery.[5] Rather than arguing against engagement with the secular concerns of her present material world, Wheatley argued for the absence of a separation between the civil and the religious, especially in relation to liberty, for which civil and religious exercises are "so inseparably united, that there is little or no Enjoyment of the one without the other."[6] This political theory and theology are far removed from Hammon's concepts of religious duty, civic disengagement, and full rejection of materialism. This philosophy fell more in line with traditional Calvinism in the sense of political engagement, but it was inflected with a liberationist theology that rejected assumptions about the legitimacy of slavery in a Christian context.

Hammon's response to Wheatley's writings represents a distinct exchange of ideas and an attempt to define the world. However different the two poets' perspectives may have been, their writings, examined in relation to one another, represent a moment of negotiation of the ideals regarding the proper relationship between God and society. Within the traditions of transatlantic slave-keeping society, such communications in writing had been rare, and a self-defining society of African peoples was antithetical to the rules and often the laws of maintaining human chattel. Writing and communicating thoughts could be considered acts of resistance, as literacy was considered a measure of one's status in early America and the exchange of ideas among slaves was doubly dangerous to an economic system that required them to be disconnected from any sense of common language, history, or society that might provide a means for self-definition and organization. The religious tradition Hammon and Wheatley shared played as large a role as writing did in instigating the very public communication between them. While they did not agree on particulars, they enjoyed the common ground of Christianity and the resulting debate on the ethics of the Christianized slave. The debate was intellectual as well as social and political, and it ultimately became the lingua franca of black Christians struggling to form communities, institutions, and mass movements that would help push American slavery into the dustbin of history.

Jupiter Hammon died a slave. Phillis Wheatley died free, in large part as a result of her writings and the international attention they generated. The two writers instigated and contributed to larger conversations about slavery and the nature of human dignity on both sides of the Atlantic Ocean. Proceeding from their example, other authors showed how the language of Christianity could further organize and help to build institutions and movements that would combat the social and economic traditions of slavery and emergent racial oppression.

Religion and Resistance

Resistance occurs when something ought to be resisted. No successful organized resistance occurs without principles that enable a group to unify and operate in a directed way. The first institution to give slaves and other black people the principles for organizing effectively against the oppressive forces that dominated every aspect of their lives was religion—in particular, sanctioned practices of Christianity. The patterns of discontent that led to attempted insurrection most often followed the rise of religious activity in slaveholding regions.[7] Christianity gave these enslaved African-descended peoples something that masters wanted to deny: a sense of common identity and purpose that created the conditions for organization and collective action.

Black evangelicals, whom slaves believed to be sanctioned by God, became the natural leaders of these groups and communities, which depended on the evangelicals' learnedness. No institution has enjoyed more widespread success among African Americans than what has become known as the "black church."[8] By the 1770s, African and African American peoples began separating from British-American religious institutions to form congregations.[9] The indignities of racism and white domination often drove black congregants to build their own churches, but historians often overemphasize this factor in the creation of African American religious institutions. Initiative and the need to incorporate different worldviews and practices into Christian worship lay at the center of the formation of these new congregations. Whereas slavery as an institution depended largely on stripping away social, cultural, and individual identity as a means of control, the gradual development of an African American Christianity provided the context and freedom for Africans and their descendants to establish new communal ties. Establishment of such ties helped to undermine the practice of slave keeping and allowed Africans in America to retain much of their cultural heritage by incorporating African religious traditions into Christianity. Such retentions include outward physical expressions of spirituality through greater emphasis on rhythmic movement, linguistic expression, call and response, and song as well as spirit possession and remnants of the ring shout.[10] The known practice of these traditions that survived the Middle Passage and generations of enslavement points toward an alternative set of religious practices that informed and influenced African American forms of worship and interpretation in the late eighteenth and early nineteenth centuries. Indeed, these practices retained by many African peoples in North America may well have influenced common outward spiritual expressions among evangelical whites during the mid–eighteenth century revival period.[11] However, these markers of what came to be known as enthusiasm were not singular to traditional African experience (except in specific form) but were also synchronous with the enthusiastic practices of European and European-American Christians, thereby allowing for intercultural exchange of religious forms and outward physical expressions of Christian faith.

As Africans and African Americans began slowly to accept Christianity, they reshaped it into a form that better suited their particular situations as displaced peoples living in a new land. Along with what they learned from missionaries and read from the Bible, slaves incorporated into their adopted religion practices retained from African belief systems. From the start, enslaved Africans and many of their North American descendants differed substantially from European missionaries in viewing religion's role in daily life. The imported Africans saw no separation of the religious from the secular, a worldview that contributed to the delay in mass conversions. A religion that explained their temporal situation as the will of the divine, supported their enslavement, and promised only otherworldly rewards was not appealing. Many descendants of these African-born peoples who converted to traditionalist Calvinist Christianity quickly began rethinking the apolitical religion delivered to them by European proselytizers, arriving at theological positions that came to play a large role in connecting resistance to Christian duty in temporal terms. This intellectual and spiritual movement was further aided by the aggressive proselytizing and the institutional structures of the Methodist and Baptist movements; one group was sympathetic to the slaves' suffering, and the other permitted the existence and spread of independent congregations without restrictive institutional controls.

This book explores two themes, the first of which is the initial widespread and organized intellectual movement among African Americans. African American evangelical writers appropriated the language of Christianity and transformed it to establish a common ground on which to speak about social and political rights. In so doing, these writers spread the principles that enabled slaves and free blacks to form communities and thus resist oppression.[12] These African American writers attempted to find a discourse into which they could enter and assert their arguments. Christianity offered one means of accomplishing this task, and they cast their complaints and suggestions in religious terms that provided these authors with both agency and credibility as authoritative voices within the highly politicized print culture of British America and England. Thus, this book relies on an understanding of Christianity's importance in the lives of most people living in North America during the eighteenth and nineteenth centuries. By the eighteenth century, America had become a large, diverse collection of colonies representing multiple ethnicities as well as economic and political interests. Many of those interests were more or less compatible; many were not. But almost all inhabitants of the British-American colonies shared a Christian heritage that permeated nearly every aspect of their lives and served as a foundation for their overall sense of ethics.

The tropes of Christianity therefore enabled arguments against slavery and oppression otherwise ignored in British and British-American culture. Christian language and principles also helped consolidate and establish African Americans as an empowered societal group with legitimate institutional support. By the middle of the eighteenth century, black evangelicals realized the liberating potential of Christianity and began rallying African Americans around firmly established religious principles that British-American society accepted; at the same time, these evangelicals also promoted the establishment of separate religious institutions that permitted blacks to organize and consolidate social and economic power. Worshipping separately also enabled African Americans to strengthen community ties by linking their adopted religion to narratives of Africa and history in ways not open to them in the dominant British-American religious institutions. Many of the writings of the authors investigated in this book link Africans and African Americans to biblical history and legitimize black institutions and expression.

The second theme of this book concerns the overtly political nature of black institution building. The growth and broad cultural significance of black Christianity and its institutions in North America helped to lead to a liberal shift in mainstream Christianity and secular politics. By the beginning of the nineteenth century, black congregations had become so large and so influential that they were being called on to aid local governments in times of crisis. During the 1793 yellow fever epidemic in Philadelphia, for example, city leaders enlisted Richard Allen's congregation to help aid the sick and transport the dead. Black churches also served as locations for abolitionist meetings and as schools for black children. In addition to central meeting places for worship, black churches became sites for discussions of social and political matters. Black churches and the organizations they launched became central to local communities and increasingly influenced public welfare and policy.

This volume examines the literature of African American evangelical writers to discover how these works contributed to resistance movements against slavery and white domination while operating within a Christian discourse community. I examine the interracial and interethnic aspects of religious and political developments in North America but focus on primary texts by black writers and the distinctively African and Afro-British contributions to American social and political culture. Past scholars have often tended to reference black writers only to show that eighteenth- and nineteenth-century African Americans indeed had the capacity to write and thus possessed humanity. But this "head count" approach to African American literary studies and figures becomes mere tokenism in a post-civil-rights era where the need to prove one's humanity is no longer a priority. Ideology and intellectual movements therefore need to become central to contemporary studies of African American literature and culture. An approach that features black people's institutional development and use of ideology in a generally hostile context leads to a better understanding of the work the literature did as it was published, circulated, and consumed by a diverse transatlantic readership. This approach also moves the language of discussion for these early black writers and the people they represent from a "slave" or linguistic paradigm "based on the notion of inherent (and inheritable) African inferiority" to a language of survival, influence, heroism, and triumph.[13] Transatlantic black and white communities shared the institution of Christianity: black writers used Christian belief systems to argue for, build toward, and fight for freedom and full citizenship.

The primary texts examined and evaluated in this volume are not read through a single theory or theoretical position. Rather, I use several historical and theoretical paradigms as points of departure for explaining how the various texts were situated, how they circulated, and how they operated within their period. I receive extensive scholarly support and conceptual framing from Orlando Patterson's *Slavery and Social Death* (1982), which describes the processes and psychology of slave-keeping societies. Because slavery, race, and white domination are ideological systems working to sustain an overarching economic program, his theoretical insights into the operation of slave systems help to provide an understanding of the means by which black Christian evangelism disrupted and undermined oppressive practices.

I use the term *African American* to designate the large group of African-descended people born in America. However, I also use *African American* and *black* interchangeably. Some ideologies advocate the use of one term over the other. Some people prefer *black* because of its connection to the early history of civil rights struggle. Others prefer *African American* in part because it designates both an ethnicity and a national or diasporic identity. Some reject *African American* for the same reason, preferring the "racial" connotation that *black* continues to signify. By using both *black* and *African American*, I collapse the ideological boundaries that stand tentatively between the two terms and validate both of them as signifiers of civil rights, egalitarianism, and ethnicity and as a political category. This book works toward an understanding of the history of civil rights struggle and resistance. *African American* also signifies the particular experiences of African-descended people on the American continent, while *black* connects the particular experiences of African Americans to the common struggles of a diasporic community of African peoples throughout the world, an important element in examining the works of African peoples in a transatlantic context.

I use the term *British American* to signify the dominant group of settlers who occupied the North American continent prior to the American Revolution. I refer to this group as *revolutionaries* and *Americans* after 1775, when these people began separating from England to form independent governments and ultimately the United States. Many African-born peoples and their descendants fought on the side of the rebellion; I refer to members of this group as *black revolutionaries*, in large part because their goals were somewhat different and more idealistic than those of the white revolutionaries. While white revolutionaries fought for freedom from land and trade restrictions, taxes, and tariffs, black revolutionaries fought for freedom from bondage and for social equality.

I adopt Vincent Carretta's term, *Afro-Briton*, to refer to Africans and African-descended peoples who were born in or who immigrated to England. The term becomes useful in studies of those individuals, such as John Marrant, who construct an identity for themselves as Britons and British citizens. This distinction is important because many of these men fought against the Americans during the revolution or became directly involved with British politics in England. While race could be used as an identifying category, doing so would be inconsistent with the way they constructed themselves as British citizens first and foremost, never identifying themselves with the peoples or continent of North America.

Until recently, scholars studying African American literature have tended to ignore or dismiss the importance of Christian discourse in the poetry and prose of many black writers. Scholars sometimes even claimed that the only contribution some evangelical speakers and writers made to the literary tradition lay in the fact that they were black and they wrote. But ignoring the use of Christian language and ideologies for a scholarship of representation results in an uncritical discourse of tokenism. Also, the assumption that someone may be considered part of a cultural tradition solely on the basis of race participates in an essentialism that evacuates politics and responsibility from issues of identity. Only recently have scholars begun to make connections between black evangelical writers and their thoughtful conversations with each other and with British-American leaders. Many eighteenth- and nineteenth-century black evangelicals made considerable reputations for themselves through writings that called into question issues of slavery and emancipation; therefore, one aim of this book is to clarify the impact and importance of African American literature on publishing and on the public consciousness of the time.

Closely related to the fact that black evangelicals knew of and utilized the power of print to make their arguments is the centrality of their work to contemporary discussions and the influence of their work on later writers in the tradition. While many of the poems, sermons, books, and narratives examined in this volume fell into obscurity between the years of Reconstruction and the late 1970s, at the time of their publication they were often hot commodities that were widely read and therefore had significant impact on the public conscience. *A Narrative of the Lord's Wonderful Dealings with John Marrant* (1785) would have been considered a best seller on both sides of the Atlantic by today's standards. And the fact that Thomas Jefferson felt it necessary to give a negative review of Phillis Wheatley's *Poems on Various Subjects, Religious and Moral* (1773) in his *Notes on the State of Virginia* (1784) indicates, among other things, that her book was being read and discussed by powerful political and public figures.

In a culture that seriously incorporated religion into its understanding of society and politics, giving slavery and emancipation moral and religious significance granted the issues much more popular appeal. William J. Scheick has observed that writers such as Wheatley "participated in the African American tradition of using scripture as materia medica, as a therapeutic means of revising and transforming social reality."[14] However, while some early black writers took a gentle approach to changing social reality, others were more direct. For example, David Walker's *Appeal to the Coloured Citizens of the World* (1829), meant for the ears of slaves and friendly white abolitionists, so disturbed southern slaveholders that they enacted laws banning the book and its distribution and pressed for stronger enforcement of slave codes. Numerous other evangelical texts also influenced the American religious and political scene between 1760 and 1835. This book continues the work of uncovering and exploring the impact of African American religious writing on the general culture of North America.

Many scholars of black literature writing roughly between 1960 and 1985 looked for the resistant moves in African American texts, searching for the moment when the author cried out explicitly against slavery and oppression. These scholars were often disappointed when they did not find the direct challenges characteristic of later, more contemporary activists. Such an approach undermines any real understanding of the nature of oppression in an eighteenth- and nineteenth-century context. Even when resistance to British-American oppression is present, it is often overlooked because it is articulated in a religious idiom or theological principle that is all too easily dismissed simply as acquiescence to white hegemony. Once again, oppression becomes the center of the discussion in these instances, while black intellectualism remains uninvestigated. This mistake happens even in cases where the text under question generated controversy at the time it emerged.

Further, approaches focusing on religious formalism are useful guides in the explication of these works by black authors, and resistance may be found there, but understanding the religious context in which those forms arose and flourished sheds light on the ways that the people of the period reacted and responded to those forms through writing. Formalist approaches often map white discourse onto black bodies, even when discussing slave narratives as spiritual biographies, as a result of the perpetuation of the Eurocentric idea of black bodies as savage, untamed blank spaces open for inscription, definition, and categorization. For example, the eminent German philosopher G. W. F. Hegel uses Africa as the symbol for absence in *The Philosophy of History* (1837). In the introduction, he speaks of the continent as emblematic of absence, without history, as outside the boundaries of history and void of any traces of what constitutes civilization. In Hegel's philosophy, "Negroes" live "in a completely wild and untamed state," and the fundamental characteristic of Africans is a "perfect contempt for humanity."[15] He makes these claims and philosophical propositions regardless of the fact that the African continent was a vast land with a diverse population featuring vibrant cultural and historical traditions.[16] Thus, white perceptions of Africa, black bodies, and black literary works are often described in terms of absence—of culture, civilization, and merit—until white intervention supplied these qualities. But Africans and African Americans were already fully formed and cultured individuals and groups who necessarily had to adapt a variety of ethnic traditions to the demands of a new social milieu. The forms of religious worship are not merely holdovers from a vague memory of African traditions but rather part of a meaningful negotiation and reinterpretation of social reality and its contexts.

Some observers argue that part of the process of making a slave was disconnecting the individual from any shared sense of community or heritage within which to contextualize and understand the present. Individual slaves certainly had pasts, but "a past is not a heritage. Everything has a history, including sticks and stones."[17] Masters sought to disconnect their property from a sense of belonging to any legitimate social order other than that of bondage. Slavery, therefore, depended on desocializing slaves, making them no better than sticks and stones and not even as good as livestock. As Patterson has elaborated, "Slaves differed from other human beings in that they were not allowed freely to integrate the experience of their ancestors into their lives, to inform their understanding of social reality with the inherited meanings of their natural forebears, or to anchor the living present in any conscious community of memory."[18] Turning human beings into slaves meant disconnecting and disassociating those people from their social, cultural, and familial pasts, thus negating what made them individuals. Changing the names of slaves from the names given to them from long tradition among their people to some form of an English diminutive was to "consign them to a perpetual childhood" as unsocialized people. By giving slaves names akin to barnyard animals "as if to represent their distance from humanity" and omitting surnames, slave owners obliterated slaves' lineages and adulthoods.[19] The elimination of names that held social significance and their replacement with names that lacked meaning or were diminutives formed an initial part of the desocialization of humans from their pasts, from their birthright.

The denial of free worship continued the process of indoctrinating people into slavery. Although individual slaves brought with them the beliefs and practices of their homelands, exercise of these traditions was prohibited and often punished. In the place of time-honored practices, slaves received a Christianity often mediated by slavers and ministers who advanced the religion's compatibility with perpetual servitude. Christian ministers often sought to resocialize slaves to believe in their innate inferiority according to biblical readings provided by the clergymen. Africans and African Americans remained historically and religiously inferior subjects as long as their captors kept them illiterate and restricted their understanding of the Scriptures used to explain slaves' place in the universe.

The "socialized death" of Africans in the slave system may to some extent have helped to transform a person into a slave but could not completely eradicate the memories, will, and lifeways of the first generations of African Americans grappling to maintain a link with their roots. Far from docile and accepting, Africans generally chose not to adopt Christianity for nearly the first two centuries they were in North America. In fact, the vast majority of African and African American slaves living in the British-American colonies were born and died with almost no knowledge of Christianity.[20] The lack of trained ministers and the large number of slaves presented an obstacle for Anglican missionaries to the continent, as did the unwillingness of many of those ministers to spread the Gospel to resistant slaves who held onto traditional beliefs and practices.[21] Slaves who resisted found a bleak and demeaning religion that emphasized their inferiority far from appealing: it had no connection to their temporal conditions except in the most negative of terms.

Not until the middle of the eighteenth century, around the time of the first and second Great Awakenings, did transplanted Africans and African Americans begin to adopt Christianity. Certain Christian traditions began to take on characteristics familiar and relevant to these African peoples, who thus became more able to incorporate traditional forms of worship and expression into their adopted religion, transforming it. During this time of rising literacy, African Americans developed messages and forms of worship that addressed the difficulties of life as well as the nature of the human spirit in terms more reflective of their social reality. As Beverly M. John has noted, "Slaves did not have hegemonic power, but they did have the ability to assign meanings and symbols in a fashion that was totally disparate from the meanings and symbols assigned by those who devaluated them. So enslaved blacks created a culture that imposed the ideological foundations of the various African cultures from which they descended on the objective conditions in which they were located and, thus, created a hybrid culture to meet the needs in the antebellum period."[22] What appealed to the enslaved was not the distilled Christianity that early missionaries had tried to impose as a means of social control; rather, they preferred and converted to the more open Christianity of the evangelical period of the mid–eighteenth century, which offered possibilities for interpreting life experiences within the context of a religion of hope rather than as a bleak justification of and rules for their current condition.

As an example, the benne seed ritual of the Gullah people in the South Carolina low country exemplified the African cultural beliefs incorporated into a North American black Christian reality that reflected their condition and mores. An element of this ritual included transforming the idea that informing on a fellow slave who stole from the master was a sin. Instead, informing on an enslaved colleague became a sin, undermining the collective community values of the enslaved group. Slaves recognized the inherent injustice of perpetual slavery and the poverty the system forced on the community. Practiced under the guise of the Baptist faith, this revision of Christian dogmatism took into account the context of community interest over absolutism about the definition of sin, particularly in relation to the temporal master-slave relationship.[23] Far from being immoral on the subject of theft, slaves took a very serious attitude toward it within the group, considering stealing from other slaves a breach of trust, but "felt no compunctions about such acts directed toward the slave system."[24]

For the enslaved Africans of the seventeenth and early eighteenth centuries, conversion en masse was never a simple matter of being drawn to the kinesthetic elements of Christian revivalism or a need to be overseen by the presence of a providential, overruling deity (a role already filled by temporal masters). Instead, enslaved Africans were drawn to a combination of kinesthetic and ideological potentials that mid- and late-eighteenth-century revivalism offered. Innumerable African Americans gained the ability to worship more independently, transforming traditional forms of European Christianity into a more egalitarian, hybrid religion that would contribute to transforming Christian practice in general as well as become the foundation for black culture and political activity. This theology and religious practice would become more African in character as black Americans began, as Patterson has said, to "integrate the experiences of their ancestors into their lives" and to "inform their understanding of social reality" in an active, productive way.[25]

Since Christianity was such an influential basis for organizing life and the language by which interethnic communication could take place, African Americans used their religion to transform social reality, to argue for social and political rights, and to bring together communities capable of building institutions that could resist oppression. Three assumptions undergird my position. First, Christianity played a much larger role in early black resistance movements than scholars have realized. Second, black Christianity operated and spread throughout the transatlantic as a consequence of an understanding of the power of the spoken and written word to encourage positive change by black speakers and writers. Third, African American literature and culture was not marginal in the sense in which contemporary literary criticism uses the term. Blacks' writings and speeches constituted a significant part of mainstream culture and played an important role in changing the religious and political ideals and practices of the time.

The conventional wisdom remains, however, that Christianity served as a tool to domesticate slaves. While many ministers and evangelicals bent on spreading Christianity certainly made this claim, among many others, for the most part the reality was very different. According to Sylvia R. Frey and Betty Wood,

"Sketchy though it is, the evidence clearly disproves the notion that the Christianization of slaves was a weapon wielded by planter-slaveholders to make their bondpeople more pliant."[26] In reality, planters generally refused to allow their slaves to engage in Christian worship in the belief that knowledge and practice of the Gospels would "ruin" the slaves and make them no good as servants. Many planters heavily invested in the economics of slavery realized the liberatory potential of Christian theology and practice. Slaveholders perceived that baptizing slaves would result in their loss as property, since only the heathen could be rightfully enslaved.[27] However, as blacks became more conversant in Christianity, they realized that Christianizing slaves meant socializing them in a way that would allow them to argue convincingly for their liberation.

These ideas about the nature of Christianity did not spring forth without precedent. Christianity may have been one of the organizing principles of British royal and ecclesiastical authority, but that authority had been challenged many times by radical and enthusiastic Christian movements that appealed to the British underclasses. At various times, poor Britons had adapted and used Christianity to argue against their disenfranchisement. As a result, missionaries connected to the Anglican tradition and the British government generally exercised care in preaching to Africans and African Americans to avoid conveying the idea that conversion meant temporal deliverance from their condition as slaves. Slaves were free only in a spiritual sense, and white missionaries highlighted this theology in their lessons to blacks. In response, slaves resisted widespread conversion to a religion that supported their demoralized status as chattel servants and in some cases even abandoned portions of the Bible, particularly the Pauline texts that white ministers often cited as proof of slavery's compatibility with Christianity.

Cotton Mather, for example, was one of the earliest and most influential apologists for slavery writing in British North America, arguing, "It is come to pass by the *Providence* of God, without which there comes nothing to pass, that Poor Negroes are cast under your government and protection."[28] Drawing his theology principally from Pauline texts, Mather argues, "What *Law* is it that Sets the *Baptised Slave* at *Liberty*? Not the *Law of Christianity*: that allows of *Slavery*. . . . *Christianity* directs a *Slave*, upon his embracing the *Law of the Redeemer*, to satisfy himself, *That he is the Lord's Free-man*, tho' he continues a *Slave*. It supposes . . . [t]hat there are *Bond* as well as *Free*, among those that have been *Renewed in the Knowledge and Image of Jesus Christ*."[29] While this reading of Colossians 3:11 may be a stretch, it is nevertheless a valid interpretation given St. Paul's general ambivalence toward the subject of slavery throughout his epistles.[30]

Prior to the Great Awakening, the theological mantra held that Christianity needed to be spread to the slaves but that conversion and baptism did not under any circumstances change their legal status as slaves. "As St. *Paul* has expressly told us, I *Cor.* Vii. 20. where he is speaking directly to this very Point," states Edmund Gibson, the lord bishop of London, "*Let every Man abide in the same Calling, wherein he was called*; and at the 24th Verse, *Let every Man wherein he is called, therein abide with God.*" This passage clearly indicates that this bishop saw slavery as a legitimate practice within Christian society.[31] Gibson wrote to the British plantation owners of the various American colonies, admonishing them for resisting the efforts of active missionaries. Plantation owners were well aware of the revolutionary potential of the Christian message and much of the literature in the Bible. They did not want their slaves to have access to the ideals of Christian salvation, which could have disastrous results for slave-keeping society's cultural and economic system, but Gibson clearly addresses their concerns. "It is further pleaded," the lord bishop argues, "that the instruction of Heathens in the Christian Faith . . . would destroy both the Property which the Masters have in them . . . and that making them Christians only makes them less diligent, and more ungovernable."[32] In response, echoing Mather in *The Negro Christianized*, Gibson replies that "the embracing of the Gospel, does not make the least Alteration in Civil Property, or in any of the Duties which belong to Civil Relations" and that the real reason for slaves' inability to be governed is their want of religion, deprived by their masters.[33] Church leaders generally wanted to Christianize slaves but encountered resistance not only from the masters but from the slaves as well.

Despite missionaries' efforts to bring slaves into Christianity, Africans and African Americans initially resisted conversion, in large part because the types of lessons being delivered were slanted to justify slaves' degraded status as chattel. Although some blacks converted early on, biblical and ecclesiastical authority and interpretation were restricted to the traditional church hierarchy of bishops and priests, and their version of Christianity, as it was received by slaves, included the preservation of a slave-keeping status quo. Slaves resisted these interpretations of Scripture in at least two ways, refusing to convert or ignoring those portions of the Bible that were routinely presented as supporting African-descended people's status as slaves. Such passages were not meaningful to slaves' lives in any positive or productive way.

Some clerical voices argued that slavery was not protected by canon law. For example, Samuel Sewell, author of *The Selling of Joseph* (1701), was one of the best known of the early abolitionist preachers. Nevertheless, the argument for the compatibility of slavery within Christian society held supremacy institutionally and culturally, as no church organization, including the Church of England, which most influenced British North Americans, stood against human bondage. The arguments for Christological slavery also interacted in not-so-secret collusion with the economic interests of slave-keeping society. And as Margaret Creel has pointed out, early European-American Christians used biblical slavery and the slave codes to maintain a particular social order rather than to contemplate the destinies of black slaves.[34] In this sense, theology was far from separate from the economic interests of powerful members of the political structure—also, not incidentally, prime contributors to church coffers. However, once the Great Awakening took hold, a multiplicity of voices not necessarily beholden to the political and economic institutions of England or the Anglican Church began to reevaluate the old theologies and speak out against slavery as an organizational endeavor. In large part, this development resulted from the fact that black people for the first time had access to positions of authority, serving as ministers who could develop and spread new interpretations of biblical Scripture.

For Africans and African Americans living in British North America, the Great Awakening represented a watershed moment in which the spread of protestant Christianity enabled a redistribution of religious authority. Some blacks who became ministers preached as members of organized congregations or denominations, while others served as itinerant lay preachers, wandering over the North American landscape and spreading versions of Christianity that addressed the immediate physical and psychological conditions of slave and free blacks. Either way, these black clergy became the backbone of a religious and intellectual tradition, founding a movement that contributed to the presence of black voices from the pulpit in addition to serving as organizational leaders who built institutions. These institutions, both religious and secular, became the basis for African American organization against oppression in the transatlantic community.

Christianity had many facets that appealed to enslaved Africans and African Americans in British North America. Singling out one Christian perspective as *the* facet of Christianity that appealed to slaves would artificially homogenize a movement with multiple perspectives. However, one aspect of late-eighteenth-century Christianity that resonated with blacks was its message of universal equality, which allowed for a multiplicity of interpretations, both ideological and kinesthetic. In the evangelical period, this message of equality, along with the growing phenomenon of itinerant ministry, allowed black preachers to assume formal and informal leadership roles. Once large numbers of Africans and African Americans began converting to Christianity, white leaders—particularly authorized church officials and slave masters—faced a conundrum. On the one hand, blacks in the southern territories wanted to begin ministering to one another, but this practice meant that slaveholders would have to recognize these ministers as authorities or even as leaders who received their wisdom from a higher power than the masters. On the other hand, in regions without slavery, black religious leaders sometimes came into conflict with official church leaders who chose not to recognize them as social equals. Slavery and racism then stood as obstacles to the full integration of black people into mainstream Protestant Christian culture.

Organized Christian worship was allowed in southern territories only under the strictest supervision. Slave preachers and free black preachers who ministered to slaves had to provide local authorities with the contents of sermons. This requirement clearly restricted the freedom with which congregants could contemplate their relationship to God and one another, but slaves circumvented these constraints by finding safe harbors in the woods and swamps of the surrounding countryside, where they could practice unique forms of Christianity unsupervised by masters.[35] Thus, even though masters and local authorities tried to limit what black Christians could teach and believe, slaves nevertheless participated in covert forms of resistance. Further, beyond the gaze of their masters, slaves used the opportunities for worship to plan further ways to exert independence, including insurrection justified by principles of Christian idealism. So, from the very beginning, Christianity offered and inspired opportunities for clandestine resistance rather than merely serving as a tool for widespread white domination. Southern blacks' theologies also set the stage for other ways to resist in the intellectual tradition.

In the northern regions, where slavery constituted a less dominant force, other types of power struggles took place between black and white Christians, as chapter 5 more clearly shows. In the North, although many churches admitted blacks to worship services, leadership in most of the denominations was generally restricted to whites. Blacks could serve as lay preachers and exhorters but only rarely received official recognition as ministers and priests. Blacks thus eventually began to worship independently, forming church societies and organizing various types of educational and relief societies around the institution of the church. Thus, the church and its attendant theologies became unifying principles. Blacks thus created a foundation for an organized, sustained assault on the oppressive forces of both slavery and institutionalized racism. The church and a Christian theology that emphasized universal concepts of human dignity provided the basis for buttressing and explaining the cause of abolition in both the North and the South.

Africans' and African Americans' initiative and desire for free worship without supervision contributed to the development of new forms of devotion based on a variety of traditional African and European practices.[36] Christianity interacted with traditional West African religions and Islam, resulting in the emergence of a set of beliefs and practices that explained the African presence in the New World and provided the basic principles for spiritual growth and physical existence within that environment. Two central components of black culture and spirituality, orality and extemporaneous address, significantly influenced the development and spread of black Christianity. Enthusiastic and charismatic expression also played a large role in blacks' development of a divergent theology in North America that helped in organization building and the creation of a public voice with which to communicate their concerns. Enthusiastic worship was not particular to black experience but a tradition that linked black and white egalitarian Christians in many ways.

While black worship may have emphasized orality, extemporaneous address, and enthusiasm as common unifying elements, the ideological construct that has come to be known as the black church actually derives from a variety of institutional and theological perspectives. Within the context of Western philosophy, the practice of enthusiasm can be seen as early as Plato, who advocated a form of knowledge derived from divine inspiration. In the *Phaedrus*, Plato describes philosophy as a blessed type of madness, allowing Socrates to fall into trances as the divine voice speaks to and through him.[37] The people of Athens often criticized Socrates for his strange behavior.[38] But this entranced, direct communication with the divine is a kind of inspired knowledge that the Greek philosopher saw as an ideal form released from the constraints of bodily pleasure, pain, fear, and desire.[39] The city of Athens thus executed Socrates for his enthusiasm. Similarly, Friedrich Nietzsche speaks elegantly of ancient Greek Dionysian mystery cults in *The Birth of Tragedy*.

In English tradition, the earliest usage of the word *enthusiasm* cast it as "a pejorative term . . . denoting false claims to divine inspiration," and few early modern clergymen willingly admitted that the phenomenon was infecting their congregations.[40] I define *enthusiasm* not in negative terms but rather as the outward bodily and verbal expression of a real or imagined connection with a divine being. This tradition has a long history of threatening functioning social and political establishments, as it is every bit as political as it is spiritual in nature. Civic and religious authorities therefore often associate enthusiasm with the underclass, and by the early eighteenth century, the term served as a signifier of criminality, seditious behavior among the poor, and blackness. The practitioners of enthusiastic religious worship, however, perceived outward displays of enthusiasm as powerful markers of divine salvation, new birth, and even elevated spiritual and social status. The enthusiastic sects also became some of the most active proselytizing denominations. Because of these two factors, in late-eighteenth-century British North America, large segments of the white and black underclass, including slaves, attended religious denominations that encouraged enthusiastic worship. Whites and blacks often worshiped together, much to the chagrin of civil and ecclesiastical authorities.

During the classical period, Greek philosophers identified enthusiasm as a form of divine madness. But throughout the eighteenth and nineteenth centuries, the word *enthusiasm* had pejorative connotations; it was a slander toward people who professed to have a direct connection to the divine. Some of the earliest Christian enthusiasts were the Unitas Fratrum, later known as the Moravians. Founded in the fifteenth century on the belief in spiritual renewal and fellowship, these Christians renounced wealth, privilege, serfdom, and nobility as false and believed in holding property in common. They also believed that the New Testament was a "blueprint to construct a society without class, violence, or oppression."[41] Because of this movement's popularity among Bohemian peasants, civil authorities arrested and persecuted these enthusiasts for their radical beliefs.

The movement nevertheless survived, and by the eighteenth century it had abandoned its more radical ideals, such as its insistence on social equality, and adopted pietism (the rejection of religious formalism for an experiential and emotionally charged communication with the divine and salvation by faith alone).[42] This experience with the divine signified one's actual, not symbolic, connection to God.

While on a mission to Georgia between 1735 and 1738, John Wesley, one of the founders of the Methodist movement, was deeply influenced by the Moravians he encountered. He agreed with their rejection of formalism and incorporated experiential communication with the divine into his Methodist version of High Anglicanism. These new doctrines came to define Methodism in contrast to the established English church, which was not considered separate from government. Further trouble arose when Wesley began restoring the concept of social equality into his movement. Methodism grew, especially among the poor, and civil and religious authorities came to associate the movement with criminal activity.

In 1740, Gibson, the lord bishop of London, published a scathing attack on Methodism, accusing adherents to the sect of holding "unlawful assemblies" because the large crowds of poor attendees violated the Act of Toleration, passed to prevent sedition. Gibson's tract was a stern criticism of Methodism and its popularity among the poor titled *Observations upon the Conduct and Behaviour of a Certain Sect, Usually Distinguished by the Name of Methodists* (1740), which states that Methodists not only break the law by holding these large assemblies but also "have the Boldness to preach in the *Fields* and other open places, and by public Advertisements to invite the *Rabble* to be Hearers."[43] Religious authorities viewed large, emotional assemblies of the poor with suspicion, and the lord bishop warns that Methodism's appeal arose of the "strange notion" among the leaders of the movement "'*That . . . our Saviour is,* NOW, *about gathering his Sheep out of all Nations, out of all Professions, out of all Parties, out of all national Churches; into* little *Flocks which he governs with his* Word *and* Spirit.' A Notion which must be considered by all sober and uninfected Minds as merely *Enthusiastical.*"[44] He further spells out the threat to civil authority, arguing that "the same exalted Strains and notions . . . tend to weaken the *natural* and *civil* Relations among Men, by lending the Inferiors, into whose Heads those Notions are infused, to a Disesteem of their Superiors . . . [t]hough those Superiors are otherwise sober and good Men, and regular Attendants of the Ordinances of Religion."[45] The lord bishop is concerned primarily with two problems: enthusiastic religion (1) threatens real religion by appealing to the passions of the lower classes and by failing to conform to national laws and (2) is doctrinally dangerous because it leads the lower classes toward the belief that the individual wields equal religious authority with his social superiors and thus contributes to an ideological breakdown of the class system.

The lord bishop's concerns regarding civil and ecclesiastical authority were not new or unique. Christian evangelicals all the way back to Paul have found enthusiasm suspect, and people in positions of authority have always been wary of it. Enthusiasm, therefore, has a long tradition of being regarded a threat to both traditional religion and the state. Gibson therefore calls on his readers to pursue a more reasonable observation of religion, arguing that public worship is better observed by "regular Attendance . . . by good Men in a serious and composed Way" than "by those sudden Agonies, Roarings, and Screamings, Tremblings, Dropping Downs, Ravings, and Madness" of the seditious Methodists and their flocks of the poor.[46]

By the mid–eighteenth century, the British North American wing of the transatlantic religious revival known as the Great Awakening was in full swing. Wesley was among the many itinerant evangelists whose teachings spread to British North America, and his movement attracted whites and blacks alike. The "Agonies, Roarings, and Screamings" and general "madness" described by the lord bishop of London apparently also formed a part of North American evangelism, as evidenced by one indignant observer's description of a Methodist camp meeting:

> Here ought to be considered too, a most exceptional error, which has the tolerance at least of the rulers of our camp meetings. In the *blacks'* quarter, the coloured people get together, and sing for hours together, short scraps of disjointed affirmations, pledges, or prayers, lengthened out with long repetitious *choruses.* . . . With every word sung, they have a sinking of the of one or other leg of the body alternatively; producing an audible sound of the feet at every step, and as manifest as the steps

of actual negro dancing in Virginia &c. If some in the meantime sit, they strike the sounds alternatively on each thigh. . . . [T]he evil is only occasionally condemned and the example has already visibly affected the religious manners of some whites.[47]

A more sympathetic but nevertheless skeptical white observer described another black church meeting:

As soon as I had taken my seat, my attention was attracted by an old negro near me, whom I supposed for some time to be suffering under some nervous complaint; he trembled, his teeth chattered, and his face, at intervals, was convulsed. He soon began to respond aloud to the sentiments of the preacher, in such words as these: "Oh, yes!" . . . Sometimes the outcries and responses were not confined to ejaculations of this kind, but shouts, and groans, and terrific shrieks, and inescapable expressions of ecstasy. . . . I was once surprised to find my own muscles all stretched, as if ready for a struggle—my face glowing, and my muscles stamping—having been infected unconsciously.[48]

Scholars suggest that the enthusiastic worship of early black Christians constituted a retention of traditional West African worship practices that featured ecstatic dance movement and spirit possession.[49] Indeed, this is very likely the case, as many eighteenth- and nineteenth-century observers comment on the ecstatic behavior of black congregations during Christian worship, particularly the seemingly alien nature of the dancing and the incorporation of the ring shout into meetings. However this theory does not account for enthusiastic worship practices among many European Christians long before any significant contact with descendants of West Africa. These enthusiastic practices were popular impulses that appealed to blacks as activities predicated on resistance—compatible with the inherently populist, revolutionary nature of Protestant Christianity. Enthusiasm was popular for precisely the reasons established religious authorities were wary of it—it is a physical expression of an ideological challenge to class and race systems within traditional ecclesiastic and civil institutions. Just as Socrates' "divine voice" challenged a corrupt Athenian polity, enthusiasm threatened traditional church and civic values, particularly in England and early British North America, where the cultures were tremendously stratified by class and race. The poor, the Dissenting, and the enslaved therefore constitute the "rabble" attempting to redefine the hierarchical relationship between God and humanity and by extension the social order. And as was the case with most radical social movements, numerous observers described enthusiasm as an "infection."

This form of divine madness so appealed to both blacks and poor whites in England and British North America because people needed a sign of their relationship to divinity. People who participated in the more emotional sects, like Methodism, saw enthusiasm as an outward sign of closeness to sainthood and divinity. Unlike earlier and more orthodox Calvinists, these Christians saw emotionalism, rather than material wealth or status, as a legitimate sign of piety. This belief in the role of enthusiasm was a potent rhetorical tool, empowering traditionally oppressed peoples such as slaves, the British underclass, and poor British Americans. In fact, not until the late eighteenth century, when enthusiasm became a feature of Christian doctrine in some movements, did Africans and African Americans begin to adopt the religion. African-descended peoples viewed enthusiasm not merely as emotion but as a condition that connected the redeemed with one another and the divine. Enthusiasm in Christianity certainly presented Africans with familiar forms of worship but took on different meanings in the new social context and began to serve as an indicator of spiritual as well as social equality with worldly masters. And with African Americans at the absolute bottom of the social chain, enthusiasm remained an integral part of black worship, while white acceptance of the practice would diminish as racial distinctions became more socially and politically pronounced.

The Baptist and Methodist movements were particularly popular among blacks during the Great Awakening, attracting much larger numbers than other denominations for several reasons. First, both were highly mobile proselytizing denominations. While other sects might have sought new converts, Methodist and Baptist ministers and congregants traveled vigorously over multiple geographic regions to spread the Word. Second, these active proselytizers did not restrict their message to a single race but generally shared their beliefs with both black and white audiences. Since Baptists and Methodists did not usually discriminate along these lines, their message tended to be more egalitarian and less a gospel of control that emphasized the legitimacy of slavery and God's approval or sanction of the degraded social position of individuals, particularly slaves. In fact, whereas missionaries of other denominations neglected slaves, Baptist and Methodist proselytizers actively sought out bondspeople for conversion. Third, advocates for slavery saw Methodism as openly hostile to the institution. The Methodist movement had two branches during the Great Awakening, one led by Wesley and the other headed by George Whitefield. Both factions vigorously sought to convert blacks, although Wesley's branch promoted the complete abolition of slavery while the Whitefield branch was more moderate, allowing for the existence of slavery but advancing the amelioration of brutalities in the practice. Both groups emphasized itinerant ministry, pietism, and outward emotionalism and reached free and enslaved blacks throughout North America, converting large numbers to Christianity. Finally, both the Baptist and the Methodist traditions allowed African Americans to assume preaching, proselytizing, and leadership roles, thereby contributing to the burgeoning of black intellectualism and institution building, particularly in northern regions where slavery was less prevalent and where blacks had more access to literacy and more liberty to assemble to conduct affairs without white supervision.

Although Methodism spread throughout both the northern and southern regions of North America, institutional Methodism had greater success in the North while Baptism carried more influence in slaveholding southern territories. Methodism was a more organizationally structured tradition: individual churches, congregations, and preachers recognized an institutional hierarchy and answered to an association of ministers and bishops as part of a network, resulting in strong and influential institutional ties after northern black Methodism became a separate institution. Baptism, conversely, placed absolute authority on the individual churches and congregations. No institutional ties necessarily existed among congregations, and no authorities necessarily existed outside of the individual church leaders. Within the context of a strict slave-keeping society, this method of organization allowed blacks, particularly slaves, to assemble and worship, but slave masters could more easily keep such congregations and their leaders under surveillance. The Baptist model of church organization also did not overtly allow for institutional networks that could lead to mass movements or to the sharing and adoption of ideals and practices that could disrupt the slave system. Baptism thus seemed like less of a threat. Nevertheless, both enthusiastic faith traditions provided a foundation for black organization and intellectualism that would ultimately contribute to resistance movements against slavery at many levels.

While Africans and African Americans may have been drawn to Baptist and Methodist movements, these adopted forms nevertheless changed under the influence of African and African American leaders and congregations and continued to do so as a consequence of social and cultural traditions in the various regions of the Americas. Just like the traditional forms of European Anglicanism that dominated the northeastern colonies, black churches changed, often incorporating new ideas into older forms or establishing entirely new movements as social and political conditions changed within and around the institutions.

Evangelism and Resistance in the Black Transatlantic, 1760–1835 examines the question of how black evangelism developed, spread, and influenced transatlantic cultures, particularly British-American culture. I examine a variety of literary texts to determine what they reveal about the culture to which Africans and African Americans contributed so greatly, not only in economic terms (which should be obvious) but also in terms of literary and political culture. Chapter 1 follows the writing of Jupiter Hammon and charts the religious principles that he accepted and promoted as a slave who bought into much of the early lessons of a Christianity that was compatible with slavery. Chapter 2 follows the writings of Phillis Wheatley and shows her contributions to the literary tradition of the black transatlantic as the first of the African American Christian writers to articulate a theology of liberation. This chapter then shows the conflict between Wheatley's and Hammon's approaches to religion, demonstrating how two contemporaneous black slave writers situated themselves socially and historically in a Christian, slaveholding society. This chapter also explains how their views may have circulated as cultural artifacts influencing their cultural milieu. Chapter 3 analyzes the life and works of John Marrant, the first ordained black Methodist minister, whose progressive message helped set the tone for much of what would become known as the black church in North America. Chapters 4 and 5 examine the lives and writings of several black builders of institutions that contributed to the development of a black collective consciousness and African American resistance to slavery and social oppression. Chapter 6 continues the analyses of chapter 5 but focuses on Maria Stewart and her contributions to the development of distinct African American women's voices.

Evangelism and Resistance in the Black Atlantic, 1760–1835 is one effort within contemporary scholarly discourses on race, religion, and culture to attempt to map intersections between disciplines as well as to reveal the wealth of knowledge that may be gained from seriously reexamining the religious language deployed in early black American literature. The various poems, essays, speeches, and autobiographies examined in this book are far more than literary or historical footnotes. Each of these literary productions represents powerful evidence for religion and biblical exegesis as an important part of an organic African American intellectualism that ultimately contributed to institution building and organizing principles capable of resisting slavery and antiblack social injustice. This study does not provide a comprehensive study of the known literature of the period but rather offers a deeper understanding of the ways the literature of the period can be read. In addition, this book gives greater insight into the ways black intellectualism manifested itself and influenced African American as well as the larger American culture.

CHAPTER ONE

Jupiter Hammon and the Written
Beginnings of Black Theology

Jupiter Hammon made important contributions to African American writing that present contemporary readers with many problems of interpretation, particularly in the area of slave resistance. Generally neglected by literary and historical scholarship, Hammon's poetry and essays nevertheless can shed light on how black people, both enslaved and free, entered discussions concerning their destinies as human subjects in British America. In fact, Hammon's work reveals much to readers about the theological teachings slaves received about their relationships to their masters in the early to mid–eighteenth century and about how Hammon reinterpreted and spread those teachings. This chapter does not investigate whether Hammon advocated abolition; he was clearly comfortable and apparently content with his condition as a slave by the time he began publishing his writings in December 1760. Rather, this analysis reveals what is known about the religion and theological beliefs of one American slave who likely is representative of what some enslaved converts to Christianity believed about their place in the world as both slave and Christian. Hammon does not represent the thinking of all slave converts of the period, but his complex beliefs and representation of the nature of sin, belief and faith, and death and the afterlife reveal a wealth about one form of Calvinist Christianity. Many enslaved people of the time were exposed to and had the opportunity to accept or reject Hammon's conception as a way of organizing their spiritual lives and explain social reality.

In the 1990s, some scholars labeled Hammon a type of antislavery writer, arguing that his writing was emancipatory in nature, that it illustrated an enslaved human being trying to resist slavery through the language of religious literature.[1] Hammon's writings do not support this conclusion, however. Hammon was a complex individual living under unusual circumstances with certain ideological beliefs that interacted with the literary and political culture of early America, but resistance was not one of his concerns. While his occasions for writing may have held emancipatory and resistive potential, his temporal life was far from resistant, and his works ultimately validate the social and political status quo of slavery by supporting the lessons and arguments of proslavery, predestinarian Calvinist evangelists and missionaries of the period. But his writing also attempted to consolidate a community of blacks around principles of Christianity. His example would encourage and sharpen the way that black writers and thinkers debated slavery, but the message Hammon put forth was far from revolutionary. In fact, it exemplifies the traditional teachings the majority of slaves and free blacks sought to resist prior to the middle of the eighteenth century.

Hammon's writings offer today's readers access to the way in which some Christianized slaves conceived of the individual's relationship to the divine and by extension the slave's relationship to free society. Hammon thus provides a written example of the theologies slaves either rejected or remolded to fit their life experiences and needs. Though neither an abolitionist nor a black-nationalist icon, Hammon remains an important part of the literary tradition, worthy of further study for insight into transitions in early Christian doctrines from colonizing tools to organizing principles for resistance to oppression.

Hammon's writings and sermons may well indirectly have contributed, over time in his region, to black resistance by spreading common organizational principles that disrupted the desocializing effects of slavery. These principles eventually became the basis for black collective action, intellectualism, and resistance. In the hands of African Americans who would use Christianity to organize and argue against slavery, scriptural lessons and biblical exegesis profoundly affected the lives of blacks. Whether or not Hammon agreed with Christianity's effects on civil order, his participation in the spread of the religion inevitably led to future resistance movements based in large part on Christian principles. By spreading his vision of the proper Christian life, Hammon provided fuel for future black evangelical activists. But understanding his contributions to a culture of resistance requires understanding his writings within their temporal context, including the political and religious milieu and the functions of Hammon's poetry and sermons as they circulated among both white and black readers.

Hammon was not particularly interested in the end of slavery in a temporal, civil sense: such matters fell into the realm of secular politics, which did not interest Hammon except where they contradicted his sense of religiosity. In this way, he held some ideals in common with separatist Rhode Island predecessors such as Roger Williams and Samuel Gorton, both of whom believed that church and state were to operate as separate entities until they could come together as a single governing body with Scripture and a learned clergy as supreme authority.[2] As Hammon wrote in an essay directed toward black readers, particularly slaves, "I am a stranger here and I do not care to be concerned or to meddle with public affairs."[3] Although Hammon did not think in a civic-minded way and avoided mixing the religious with the secular, following the approach of most mainstream Calvinists, he was also a product of mid-eighteenth-century orthodox Anglicanism. While he rarely mentions the temporal world as anything other than a flawed intermediary stage between the Old Testament age of the prophets and the promised coming of a perfect afterlife on the Gospels, he shows some brief concern for the relationship between sin and temporal society: "My Brethren, while we continue to sin we are enemies to Christ, ruining ourselves, and a hurt to the commonwealth."[4] But Hammon's concern for the "commonwealth" comes at a time of war, and the sin, in his eyes, is the war itself—the American rebellion against England.

The elder members of the Lloyd family, who owned Hammon, owed their fortunes to commerce as merchants and were loyalist in political leaning, not interested in war with Britain or revolutionary philosophy that supported and authorized armed resistance among the American patriots. The first five decades of Hammon's life, therefore, were characterized by ideas of loyalty and subservience to the British Crown rather than ideas of independence and resistance. The political affiliations within the Lloyd family changed in 1763, when Hammon was fifty-three years old, and an American patriot, Joseph Lloyd, inherited the family manor.[5] Hammon was forced to flee along with the Lloyd family as the British marched on the town. This episode probably did not contribute to his views on patriotism or revolutionary struggle, given that the war was disrupting his sense of order and proper Christian relationships.

Hammon's views of slavery, along with other religious signposts, signal the influence of colonial Anglican traditions. At the root of Hammon's Calvinism lay a strong emphasis on an interpretation of the strict doctrine of God's complete sovereignty: God controlled everything, and if blacks lived under the yoke of slavery, then that was the will of God and would not change unless his plan called for it. Such a doctrine ran contrary to the way the majority of Calvinists thought about church, state, and themselves as citizens; however, it was perfectly acceptable as a dogma for structuring the incorporation of slaves into the larger society. So while most Calvinists saw a connection between civic activity and religion, this particular doctrine, taught to the enslaved, remained compatible with traditional master-slave relationships under the slaveholders' regime. The language of the lessons Hammon likely received from his Anglican masters, drawing heavily from the teachings of the head of the church and missionaries as well as Pauline principles, likely contributed to his views on both the relationship of religious society to civic society and the master-slave dynamic.[6] Although, as John Ashworth has shown, many Calvinist and other protestant Christians used the Bible to argue against the slavery's compatibility with Christianity by appeals to the Golden Rule and etymological arguments concerning the nature of the terms *servant* and *slave*, slavery's proponents easily refuted such arguments.[7] Antebellum literalism often got the upper hand against scholastic or historicocritical interpretations of biblical passages related to slavery and servitude. But while Hammon was certainly situated in the midst of these growing debates, he ultimately chose to accept and write in support of the school of thought, supported by his masters as well as the head of the church, that God had assigned slaves to their station and that they should look to their masters "as unto Christ," as St. Paul prescribed.[8]

Hammon's general avoidance of politics and his relative contentment with his slave status may also have reflected the fact that he was owned by a merchant family that regularly engaged in the slave trade.[9] Hammon was one of many Lloyd family slaves, and while the Lloyds may have looked at their role as masters in a paternalistic sense, they nevertheless bought, sold, and loaned out their slaves in accordance with economic expediency. Hammon may have been treated especially well, contributing to his allegiance to the family, but the specter of being sold remained ever present. His orthodox Calvinist beliefs in an arbitrary God mirrored well the master-slave relationship—the sovereign master could dispose of the slave as he pleased, just as God could save or damn any soul at his pleasure. Such a belief may underlie Hammons's emphasis on fear in "A Winter Piece" and "A Poem for Children with Thoughts on Death." Published together in 1782, the two documents exemplify Hammon's most mature thinking and writing on the subject of religion, revealing an underlying acceptance of traditionalist Calvinist views on theology that intersects with his perception of himself and other slaves in relation to the larger society.[10]

Hammon uses the word *fear* twenty-one times during his essay on the importance of repentance, thus strongly establishing the theme of his exhortation. Orthodox Calvinism firmly accepts the principle of humanity's depravity in the eyes of God. Calvinist doctrines hinge on the belief that as a consequence of the Fall of Man, human beings have no inherent goodness, and if left to their own merits, humans are destined to eternal damnation. And as Hammon notes in his essay, when penitents attempt to approach Christian salvation, "We are to come with the sense of our own unworthiness"; "We must come labouring and heavy laden not trusting our own righteousness."[11] For natural human beings, there are no good works, there is no righteousness or goodness that God is bound to observe. This sense of unworthiness plays a central role in Hammon's theology regarding his relationship with the divine. Without recognizing the individual's depravity, there can be no salvation from damnation, as one's place in the hierarchy of the saved and the damned depends on an understanding of his or her lowly nature in relation to God and Christ. However, recognition of depravity will lead humans to fear God's wrath. For Hammon, this fear signals a sincerity of spirit that will lead the unregenerate to seek an alternative to the otherwise certain penalty of damnation. Hammon perceives fear not as an irrational impulse but rather as a sign of intense rationality that children should learn as a primal impulse. "Children should be taught the fear of God," for, as Hammon quotes from Proverbs 9:10, "the fear of the Lord is the beginning of wisdom"; "children should fear the Lord."[12] No one, not even a child, is immune to human depravity, as Hammon's understanding of religion directs that all humanity is born into sin. Hammon's essay is an exhortation to the unconverted—specifically, to unconverted slaves and their masters.

The doctrine of depravity and fear that undergirds Hammon's essay closely resembles arguments made by Edmund Gibson, the lord bishop of London, who appealed to his subjects in the colonies to aid in the spread of Christianity by teaching their slaves the Gospels. In letters to both missionaries and slave owners, the lord bishop directs his readers to focus on the children of slaves, who have had the least exposure to "Pagan Rites" and share the common language of English, to save their souls from eternal damnation through knowledge of the Scriptures.[13] The lord bishop's explanation of the importance of proselytizing among slaves lacks the scriptural detail found in Hammon's essay but clearly states the Anglican Church's position on teaching Christianity to slaves. Hammon further elaborates on an existing policy laid out by the leaders of the Anglican Church. Early missionaries had difficulty persuading adult slaves to accept and convert to Christianity and thus began to target the children of slaves, who seemed more likely to convert because of the absence of language and cultural barriers.[14] Hammon's opinion on the importance of teaching slave children lessons in Christian piety may also be predicated on his own experiences, since he was born in 1711, when missionaries had great difficulty Christianizing slaves. Hammon's birth occurred just before the lord bishop issued his proclamations to his colonial subjects.

The push to focus on converting slave children may have contributed to the mid-eighteenth-century increase in the number of black people adopting Christianity. Among many other factors, this colonizing move met with both acceptance and resistance, and Hammon's essay, while mainly an exhortation to slaves, initially addresses the concerns of owners who continued to resist Christianizing their slaves: "In answer to the objectors, Sirs, pray given me leave to enquire into the state of those children that are born in those christian families, have they been baptised, taught to read, and learnt their catechism? Surely this is a duty incumbent on masters or heads of families. Sirs, if you had a sick child, would you not send for a doctor? If your house was on fire would you not strive to put it out to save your interest? Surely then you ought to use the means appointed to save the souls which God has committed to your charge, and not forget the words of Joshua, as for my house we will serve the Lord."[15] Hammon is not concerned with the legitimacy of slavery but with the overarching importance of spreading the Gospel, which was the first order for a Calvinist after conversion. Hammon provides the rationale, based on Scripture, for achieving that goal. So while church officials might seek superficial reasons and methods to convince missionaries and slave owners to Christianize slaves, Hammon finds sources for both the rationale for and the method of proselytizing slaves through his Calvinistic reading of Scripture. Hammon clearly sees slavery as a means to an end, and that end is the spread of Christianity. Quoting from Joshua 24:15, Hammon legitimizes the existence of slaves as dependents within the household of Christian masters: "As for my house we will serve the Lord."[16] These slave dependents, like all other members of the house, require proper instruction in the Scriptures to escape paganism. This is the larger lesson of Joshua 24, from which Hammon draws. The prophet Joshua has brought together all of the tribes of Israel to remind them of God's gifts to the Hebrew people and warn against the worship of false gods. Joshua delivers his cautionary message to all of the "elders," "judges," and "officers." Denied scriptural teaching, slaves are, in Hammon's estimation, like those Hebrew tribe members still predisposed to worship pagan Gods. Hammon's essay reminds masters that these slaves, who are to be considered members of the household and among the population of potential saints, require proper Christian teaching to circumvent certain damnation. As either sick children or chattel property, slaves have been "committed to [the master's] charge" by God, and the master may provide Christian teaching to save the unregenerate pagan disposed to worshipping false idols from damnation and thereby ultimately achieve a state of salvation.

By comparing slaves to the Israelites, Hammon effectively places slaves within the larger universal Christian family of the potentially elect. Joshua summoned all Israelites, including the leaders, to hear his message. Hammon's rhetorical move not only places masters and slaves on the same spiritual level but also reconfirms the social hierarchy. Hammon is concerned only with the spiritual well-being of the Christian masters and slaves, not their social status. As he places master and slave on the same plane in a spiritual sense, his temporal analogies nevertheless confirm the social hierarchy by establishing that slaves are like "sick children," not merely emphasizing the literal slave child but also infantilizing the adult slave who has not yet been brought to knowledge of God. Hammon's mollifying analogies become even more explicit when he compares the slave to a house threatened by a fire. Both houses and slaves constitute legal property under the law, and the analogy would be even more satisfying for any reader concerned with the tone and message of Hammon's essay as it addressed

Christian slave masters. So while Hammon theologically places the slave in the human family of Christians, he carefully does not imply a social equivalence between master and slave. Masters remain firmly in charge, superior to slaves in temporal terms, but have responsibilities to those souls "god has committed" to the masters' charge.[17] These temporal masters bear responsibility for teaching their slaves the fear of God, as prescribed in Joshua 24:14: "Now therefore fear the LORD, and serve him in sincerity and in truth." This passage immediately precedes the verse Hammon quotes to explain the importance of teaching Christianity to slaves. This message from the prophet Joshua certainly did not escape Hammon as he proposed his doctrine, lending further support both for the Calvinist attitude toward the proper relationship between man and God and for Hammon's emphasis on the theme of fear.

The doctrine of depravity encouraged the impulse to focus on fear as a method for proselytizing. Because God was sovereign, omniscient, and infallible and humans were depraved, limited in knowledge, and perfectly fallible, the individual had too many ways to err and end up on the receiving end of damnation—including the misperception that one was indeed of the elect. As a result, Calvinist tradition focused on fear not just as motivation but as the highest form of rationality in contemplations of God, particularly for the unregenerate. But even the regenerate saints, invited to contemplate God's love, could not be certain that they were of the elect. This uncertainty led to an anxiety regarding one's status with God. If one could not be certain, then what was one to do? How could people know, lacking infallible knowledge, if they were of the elect? Within an orthodox Calvinist sphere, people thus relied on outward signs of salvation. This phenomenon leads to Hammon's second overarching theme of "labour": "Let us now labour for that food which tendeth unto eternal life, this none can give but God only: My Brethren, it is your duty to strive to make your calling and election sure by a holy life, working out your salvation with fear and trembling, for we are invited to come without money and without price."[18] The orthodoxy of Hammon's theology concerning the election of the saints is most evident in this passage, which calls for the regenerate never to lose sight of their uncertainty. Hammon's warning here is no simple message about belief, which is never enough for the Calvinist; Hammon's message also carries no strain of Arminianism, a belief that the striving through works is sufficient to ensure salvation. Rather, the Christian life always features uncertainty concerning deliverance from damnation, and those who would be of the elect always show outward signs of that election through their daily labors as Christians, not as means to salvation but as signs of salvation. To deviate from the practices of an outward holy life would further signify one's lack of salvation, as orthodox Calvinists also believed in the perseverance of the saints. This doctrine may have helped to soften the belief in God's arbitrary selection of the elect but gave no certainty as to exactly who *was* of the elect. So, as Hammon writes in his essay, the only way to make sure one is of the elect is to labor to live a Christian life: "Therefore my Brethren, we should endeavor to walk humble and holy, to avoid the appearance of evil; to live a life void of offence toward God and towards man."[19]

However, Hammon's emphasis on the laborious nature of the Christian life gives rise to the argument that if one is genuinely of the elect, then living a holy life should not be laborious but rather should be a natural result of the individual's salvation. Given a predestinarian theology that holds chosen saints to be immune to damnation through sin, it would seem to follow that since salvation is predetermined even before birth, the chosen cannot or will not do wrong, and the Christian life is no burden to those who are naturally of the elect.

Calvinists indeed faced this problem, especially in light of the Arminian challenge that emphasized humanity's free will rather than arbitrary divine sovereignty. Hammon's essay answers this question, too. Near the end of "A Winter Piece," Hammon explains humanity's sinful nature, quoting Genesis 3:19, in which God condemns all of mankind through Adam: "In the sweat of thy face shalt thou eat bread, till thou return to the ground, for out of it wast thou taken, for dust thou art and unto dust thou shalt return."[20] Just prior to this verse, God discovers that Adam and Eve have disobeyed his commandment not to eat of the Tree of Life; humanity is consequently condemned to a life of hardship and toil. According to Hammon's theology, the proclamation of human suffering is a universal principle set forth by God. By weaving this particular section of the Scriptures into his essay, Hammon reminds his readers that just as sin is a universal impulse in humans, God's punishment for humanity's sins is also universal, extending even to the elected saints, who must also suffer the hardships of a life of labor, both physical and spiritual. In fact, the saints' perseverance through labor and sin even though they are of the elect provides others the example by which to structure their lives. As Hammon explains, "If the generality of men were more humble and more holy, we should not hear the little children in the street taking God's holy name in vain."[21]

The presence of fear and labor as themes in Hammon's Calvinist theology connects to his outward life as a slave. The ties between Hammon's temporal condition and the Calvinist teachings he received on the relationship of humanity to God could not have been lost on Hammon as he contemplated his place in the world. The life of a slave is one of fear and labor compounded by uncertainty, and such was the case in the home of the Lloyds, merchants and farmers who ran a self-sufficient estate on New York's Long Island.

While almost every commentator on Hammon remarks that he was owned by "kind masters" who "indulged" him, left unsaid is the fact that the paternalistic and "kind" Lloyds listed slaves in ledgers along with cattle and other bartered goods and chastised slaves whose behavior was deemed less than satisfactory.[22] Between 1654 and 1790, multiple generations of Lloyds spoke of their slaves in the same detached manner as the rest of their property, particularly in buying and selling human chattel. Family records repeatedly refer to the bad example other blacks set for the Lloyds' slaves, as in this note recorded by Henry Lloyd II on September 30, 1766: "Am glad to hear York behaves well. [H]e is a very sober good temper'd fellow healthy & Capable of business & believe would have been a good servant had not been hurt by the bad Example sett him by those of his Color here."[23] The Lloyd family papers mention Hammon only four times: once for being treated for "a Gouty Rhumatick Disorder," twice for his role in conveying money for the Lloyds, and finally as the recipient of "an old Saddle" as a present from James Lloyd II in 1765. Hammon's writings receive no notice at all.

In fact, the Lloyds owned a discontented slave, Opium (Obium) who receives much more attention in the family papers. After being loaned out to Henry Lloyd's father, Opium at first resists returning to the Lloyd manor house until Joseph Lloyd promises "that upon his future good behavior he may be assured of as good treatment."[24] The "kindness" of the Lloyd family may have corresponded to the behavior of individual slaves rather than to some supposed paternalistic sympathy on their part. Like most wealthy slave owners, the Lloyds considered their slaves property and appear only to have had a passing concern for their humanity.

Hammon would have certainly been familiar with their "kindness," their disfavor, and their ambivalence, all of which were certainly predicated on Lloyd family financial interests as well as on slaves' behavior. Hammon was born at Lloyd Manor, lived there his whole life, and would have seen the coming and going of other Africans and African Americans as a consequence of market transactions and estate divisions after the deaths of family members. Hammon's lived experience as a slave, subject to the whims of fate and his masters, may seem awfully arbitrary. Hammon was clearly a favorite of the Lloyd family, laboring hard to stay in the good graces of its various members. Hammon evidently succeeded, as the Lloyds entrusted him with the job of conveying money for business dealings. Such labor may have, at times, been difficult, but it ensured him a place, and he was not chastised or sold away. Hammon's actions were likely motivated as much by fear and uncertainty as by loyalty to the Lloyds, and Hammon earned himself the privilege of living in what he considered comfortable conditions.

When characterizing Hammon as a writer of resistance, almost all commentators tend to overlook the fact that African Americans within his own community clearly accused him of colluding with the white establishment to undermine efforts to end slavery. At this time, at the close of the revolution, the number of petitions and freedom suits was growing. Further inspired by the revolutionary rhetoric of freedom, slaves and free blacks actively pursued manumission and an end to the institution of slavery through the courts and state legislatures. These efforts became so numerous that they became a problem, particularly in the southern states, for slave owners dedicated to maintaining their property.[25] Sometime in or around 1782, contemporaries accused Hammon of undermining these attempts for individual freedom and the end to legal slavery.

In the middle of the exhortation in "A Winter Piece" on the necessity of fear and the importance of coming "labouring and heavy laden" to Christ, Hammon announces, "My dear Brethren, as it hath been reported that I had I petitioned to the court of Hartford against freedom, I now solemnly declare that I never have said, nor done any thing, neither directly nor indirectly, to promote or to prevent freedom."[26] Writing in 1782, Hammon was a seventy-one-year-old man whose masters clearly valued him as a servant and who may have served as a spiritual leader for other slaves. But his defense, which at first seems out of place, clearly indicates that his community included African Americans who did not trust his motives and perhaps even his spiritual message. He had, after all, personally petitioned the courts not to become free but rather to remain a slave.[27] When he writes that he has done nothing "to promote or to prevent freedom," he expressly means that he has never tried to prevent anyone else from being free, but he nevertheless does not see himself a member of a community outside the institution of slavery. Far from implying that slavery was in any way immoral, Hammon sees his master as having the duty to take care of him in his advanced age; in this view, emancipation would be immoral. While he does not argue against masters setting slaves free (rather than slaves liberating themselves by running away or otherwise being disobedient), he takes issue with the release of slaves, like himself, who wish to remain bound to their masters.

Hammon's middle and later years coincided with the Great Awakening, when substantial numbers of blacks first began to convert to Christianity as a consequence of increasing literacy among blacks, the growth of itinerant ministering, and the spread of new theologies that did not include a message of acquiescence to temporal oppression. Hammon's writing occurred during a time of transition, but his ideas had been formed while the Old Light theology remained dominant, before it began to lose ground to new attitudes about Christians' relationship to the rest of humanity. Hammon defends not only his adopted faith but also himself, as he was likely seen as a relic of an old religion that could not sustain itself in an atmosphere of radical change. By 1787, when he wrote "An Address to the Negroes in the State of New York," Hammon was facing the problem of spreading the Gospel to an audience less and less likely to turn to the orthodox Calvinist beliefs of his masters as other options and opportunities more sustaining to a defeated sense of self presented themselves. He was also facing the problem of advancing age, the implications of which clearly troubled him as he struggled to sustain the level of comfort to which he had become accustomed. As a lifelong slave with no other experience, he watched as postwar New England experienced an "unprecedented surge of emancipation sentiment."[28] In 1785, New York Quakers proposed a measure manumitting all slaves in that state; the effort culminated in the 1799 Gradual Emancipation Act.[29] The intervening fourteen years had seen fierce debate about how slavery would come to an end, with an increase in petitions for freedom and freedom suits compounding the political pressures in favor of such an act. In the midst of all this social and political upheaval—which of course followed years of open war against Great Britain—Hammon feared that he would be left without means or comfort in his old age. In his mind, to be free was to be cast adrift in uncertain waters. In "An Address to the Negroes in the State of New York," Hammon threw his rhetorical hat into the ring, seeking to make his mark on the debates.

Hammon's religious writings constituted an unusual contribution to the slavery debates raging at the time; as other African Americans petitioned courts and legislatures for freedom, Hammon preferred to argue for his continued slavery. Hammon defends himself against charges of actively petitioning against freedom in "A Winter Piece" and later contends that he supports temporal freedom for those of his brethren interested in it.[30] But his claims regarding freedom are lukewarm at best. Hammon brings his seemingly personal beliefs and concerns about freedom or the lack thereof back to the realm, attempting to support his positions. According to the theology he embraces, "all power in heaven and on earth belongs to God; if we are slaves it is by the permission of God, if we are free it must be by the power of the most high God."[31] If authorities asked Hammon his opinion about slavery and freedom, this sort of answer would have likely pleased many of Hartford's civil authorities, who would have recognized the clear orthodoxy in Hammon's statement. Hammon's religious statements illustrate that he did not oppose freedom on a theoretical level, but he also was not interested in the pursuit of it. And if the existence of slavery must be in accordance with the will of God, the slave was not entitled to question or resist.[32] God placed civil authority in the hands of white masters, who were thus entitled to decide whether to continue or abolish slavery; slaves and even free blacks must remain quiet on the matter.

Full submission is the theme of "A Winter Piece," and Hammon's attitude toward slavery in this instance as well as in his future essays is consistent with the theology of submission he represents. In fact, soon after he states his attitudes toward freedom, he exhorts his "brethren" to pray in secret for their salvation and hearts' desires rather than to perform any temporal activities that would change their civil state. They should only guard against sin, as their "delight should be in the law of the lord. . . . Let our superiors act as they shall think it best, we must resolve to walk in the steps our Saviour hath set before us, which was a holy life, a submission to the will of God. Luke xxii. 41, 42."[33] But what is the "will of God" in Hammon's worldview? It is submission to the civil order that God has put into place. Hammon's claim to being completely indifferent to civil matters ends up being disingenuous, especially with regard to slavery, as by this time in his life his theology has clear connections to the orchestration of extant civil policy.

The ambiguity of Hammon's beliefs likely resulted from his peculiar station in life as both a valued servant and a representative of his black community, a portion of which obviously viewed him with suspicion. What looks at first glance like a diversion from his original thesis on the importance of salvation actually becomes a segue into a more explicit explanation of the importance of submission to the civic status quo as a means to freedom, of the idea that continuing to labor dutifully at one's station is part of the slave's road to freedom. That is to say, a focus on salvation will lead to freedom of the soul and perhaps, if God wills it, of the temporal body.

Hammon's path through his feelings about freedom and his defensiveness against charges of supporting slavery marks a further use of the metaphor of labor in his essay. By asking his audience of slaves to submit to fear and come to Christ "labouring and heavy laden," he sets himself up for criticism from the same "brethren" that his essay is a metaphor for the legitimacy of temporal slavery. Although reasonable, this reading of his essay posed problems for the reception of his work. Predicting such a reading, he explicitly declares that he never tried to promote or condemn slavery and that he was not even interested in such public affairs, "and by this declaration I hope my friends will be satisfied, and all prejudice removed."[34] The prejudice to which he refers is the charge by other blacks that he opposes freedom movements. And the fact that he feels the need to state that he has "neither directly nor indirectly" promoted or prevented freedom implies that the suspicion that his words do, in fact, allow for the legitimacy of slavery. It is a reasonable charge. Hammon does what the apostle Paul did concerning slavery: present a very ambiguous record of his beliefs to avoid offending a powerful civil authority that could put an end to his ministry.

In Hammon's theology, laboring with heavy burdens, the efficacy of fear, a philosophy of submission, and the conditions of a slave-keeping society bore striking analogy to humanity's relationship to a sovereign, arbitrary God. While this theology also largely applied to the rest of British-American Calvinism, it outlined a stratified world. British and British-American Christians may have been slaves to God, but the Africans within their midst were their slaves as well as slaves to God, and the ruling class would use the Bible to support the legitimacy of this social order. Slavery, both as a metaphor and as temporal reality within this worldview, was a matter of scriptural understanding as well as civil law. Traditional Calvinists—particularly those with an interest in slave property— interpreted Scriptures, such as the apostle Paul's epistle to Philemon, as attesting to the legitimacy of being both a Christian and an owner of a Christian slave, since Paul sought to show that Christian principles did not negate civil laws in this matter. Abolitionists as well as slaves believed that Paul's letter to Philemon either was being misread or was not a genuine epistle of Paul's.[35] Some abolitionists argued that Philemon and Onesimus were relatives, not master and slave. Some Christianized slaves heard or read the letter and the lessons concerning it and denied that it was written by Paul or outright rejected it as Scripture. Conversely, proslavery factions saw Philemon as a clear indication of the institution's legitimacy. Proponents of slavery referred to the epistle as the "Pauline Mandate" and "adduced Philemon in support of both the institution of slavery and the dreaded Fugitive Slave Law, which required slaves in flight to be returned to their masters under penalty of law."[36] If one accepted the literalist view, as Hammon would have, that Onesimus was indeed Philemon's slave, then the proslavery reading would win and the lesson that would be drawn is that Christian slaves were expected to live within the existing social structures and serve their temporal masters as if they were rendering service to Christ.[37] Hammon does not try to say that human masters are the equivalent of Christ or God but acknowledges that the social order, in his experience and theology, is a mirror and mandate of the divine order.

Slavery's proponents would have used such literalist interpretations of biblical text to show the errors in the views of anyone suggesting that Pauline epistles argued against slaveholding. Indeed, proponents of slavery used New Testament writings to their advantage. The abolitionists trying to use Scripture to argue against slavery faced a problem: first-century Christians were not asking whether slavery was moral; it was accepted practice throughout the ancient world. Biblical writers were pondering "the way slaves were to accept their status and the way Christian slave owners were to treat the slaves in their control."[38] As Paul wrote over and over in his epistles, he and all Christians are the servants of Christ, and he never condemns the social order that practiced slave keeping. The received New Testament apostles such as Paul and Peter never overtly condemn slavery as an institution, even though the "thrust toward equality and egalitarianism" is a fundamental ideal within Hebrew tradition.[39] However, an interpretation that acknowledges this tradition requires more than literal readings of the received Bible, and as a literal-minded follower of Pauline principles, Hammon repeatedly tells readers that his personal apolitical stance on religion, which dismisses abolition as a chief concern (if any concern at all), is the proper means toward salvation. Indeed, Hammon's attitude on political engagement mirrors Paul's concerns, chiefly the spiritual. Contemporary biblical scholarship notes that within the theology of early Christendom, "Man's basic problems and needs are not political, social, or economic but spiritual, and that is the area on which Paul here concentrates."[40] Further, "We are forced to conclude that Colossians 3:22–25 reflects Paul's habitual attitude toward slaves who accepted Christianity. Contrary to what one might have expected, he was not concerned with their liberation. Within the community he took it for granted that they would show and share the love that was its most distinctive feature, but there is no hint that he did anything to change the social order. This is well illustrated by the case of Onesimus."[41] Hammon absorbed this Pauline tendency through an orthodox Calvinism imparted by his masters and consequently accepted his social position and looked forward to a heavenly future in which he no longer toiled as a slave to any human soul. But he believed that he had to remain a slave in obedience while on earth, according to the will of his masters, to become exclusively a slave to Christ in the afterlife. While abolitionists debated Paul's meaning on slavery, even going so far as to admit they might have to abandon some parts of the Scriptures, Hammon received and accepted as truth the slave masters' lessons regarding a literalist interpretation of Pauline principles on servitude.

As troubling as abolitionists may have found such literalist interpretations of Scripture, these writings and Western readers' approaches to them also resulted from generations of adjustment, as early Christian writers "accommodated the institution's contradictions by synthesizing Greek and Hebrew notions of freedom."[42] This synthesis of course led to numerous contradictions that developed over time into sophisticated arguments against human bondage within a Christian framework.[43] Hammon, however, while surely aware of these new ways of thinking about the nature of freedom and bondage within a Christian ethic, was not convinced of their legitimacy as a means to understand his personal place in the world.

Like his teachers, Hammon tends to seek answers in Scripture. He has no truck in human knowledge or logic but seeks to find the means to live in the world according to what is written in the Scriptures. In addition to the themes that drive "A Winter Piece," Hammon's work reveals a recurring emphasis on death. This preoccupation may have represented an attempt to understand the apostle Paul's eschatology in a world that had already waited nearly two millennia for the impending return of Christ. Hammon is a biblical literalist in every respect, seeming to hold a sophisticated approach to Pauline eschatology by suggesting that the Kingdom of God is one of an already existing, distant heaven accessible through death, which is a place of waiting until the return of Christ. The end of the living body and the quickly impending destiny of all humanity until that time is physical death.

A close look at Hammon's "A Poem for Children with Thoughts on Death" reveals what appears on the surface to be an ambiguous message concerning death and the third phase of biblical history, the Second Coming of Christ.[44] The first seven of the poem's seventeen stanzas are clearly written for children, as the title suggests, and Hammon draws his vision of the afterlife from Old Testament texts. In these stanzas, death is the beginning of the new age when "souls shall leap beyond the skies, / And live among the just."[45] Hammon tells children in this poem, just as he tells adults in "A Winter Piece," that time is short and that they must begin to pay attention to the state of their souls.

> Remember youth the time is short,
>   Improve the present day
> And pray that God may guide your thought,
>   And teach your lips to pray.[46]

Published with "A Winter Piece," the poem has consistent themes dealing with death, the value of spiritual wisdom, and the need for immediate repentance. But Hammon also emphasizes the eschatology of the apostle Paul. This is primarily a poem of endings. But the first seven stanzas offer a simple message to children: if they do as they ought in life, their souls will go to heaven. However, beginning with stanza 8, Hammon's explanation of death and the Second Coming becomes more sophisticated than a die-and-go-to-heaven scenario, and the poem changes to something other than a simple message to children. The last ten stanzas of the poem draw on New Testament arguments of death and the afterlife. One does not die and immediately go to a heaven or hell but remains in waiting for the Second Coming.

> Start ye saints from dusty beds,
>   and hear a savior call,
> Twas Jesus Christ that died and bled,
>   and thus preserve'd thy soul.[47]

The saints, weather children or adult, enter a state of waiting until the Second Coming, when the regenerated will be restored from death to a perfect state.

Then shall you hear the trumpet sound,
    And rend the native sky,
Those bodies starting from the ground,
    In the twinkling of an eye.[48]

Hammon's gloss of I Corinthians 15:52–54 and his explication of various Old and New Testament commentaries on death and salvation throughout "A Winter Piece" are rounded out by "A Poem for Children." Both works deal with the enduring problems that occupied Hammon throughout his life, revealing a wealth of information about how his theology affected the way he saw the world.

"A Winter Piece" and "A Poem for Children" reveal Hammon's mature theological belief system. That system shows an acceptance of traditionalist Calvinist teachings that distinguishes him as a believer in an orthodoxy that was quickly being replaced by other theologies developing under transatlantic Calvinism. A new set of civil and religious philosophies was beginning to take root in British North America, and times of change always provoke some resistance. Hammon was one of those who resisted. An understanding of his underlying theology facilitates an understanding of the religious, social, and political context of the rest of Hammon's writings, especially with an eye toward his attitudes about the changes going on around him, especially as Calvinism was being reimagined by other blacks who were also part of the transatlantic cultural tradition. Much of the rest of Hammon's written works—in particular, his other writings dating from during and after the American rebellion against the British—become clearer in light of his religious worldview.

Hammon's writing poses significant problems for those looking to read him as a proponent of abolitionism, he does not seem to endorse a radical politic of resistance against white-supremacist oppression and slavery. In fact, some of his work may be interpreted to represent slavery as a legitimate institution, authorized by the will of God. His essay, "An Address to the Negroes in the State of New York," first published in 1787, clearly argues that slaves are the legitimate servants of the British-American captors and that blacks should stop agitating for the immediate end of slavery "not only because God commands, but because our own peace and comfort depend on it."[49] It might at first glance seem drastic for a slave to espouse the idea that God commands slaves to stop agitating against slavery; however, this argument is far from radical, falling completely within the realm of orthodox Calvinist theology, which based its doctrines of slavery on various long-standing interpretations of Pauline principles of the master-slave relationship. Paul, after all, returns the runaway slave, Onesimus, to his master, Philemon, after converting the bondservant to Christianity.[50] In this instance, the apostle instructs Philemon to receive Onesimus and asks him to consider the returned man not only as a slave but also as "a brother beloved."[51] The ideas of being both a Christian and a slave owner or of being both a slave and a Christian thus do not lack precedent in the Bible, and slave owners and accommodating evangelists highlighted this compatibility. Precisely this message repelled many enslaved Africans, keeping them from embracing Christianity for almost two centuries; some converted slaves, however, found that this message reinforced and was central to their conversion into Christian society.

Erskine Peters has correctly observed that Hammon's value as a writer was as a recorder of the master-slave relationship and that his work can shed light on the intercourse between the two classes, but Peters's reading of "The Kind Master and the Dutiful Servant" as a piece of dramatic irony that reveals a "double-talking" or double consciousness on Hammon's part, demonstrating that the slave had a degree of authority and choice within the relationship, does not hold.[52] Hammon's poem offers little in the way of irony and certainly has nothing akin to W. E. B. Du Bois's double consciousness. Rather, Hammon wrote a statement on the proper slave-master relationship within the context of the American Revolution. The boundaries of this relationship are delineated by Hammon's understanding of his Orthodox Calvinist knowledge on the matter of slavery. Rather than trying to articulate a resistant identity and agency, Hammon outlines the hierarchy of humankind under God as both an interpretation of Scripture and a critique of the Revolutionary War, which he despised for uprooting him from his home on Long Island and splitting the Lloyd family.

Hammon's writings seem to promote peace and order over the struggle occurring around him in the name of liberty. His poem, "A Dialogue Entitled the Kind Master and the Dutiful Servant," written during the revolutionary conflict, clearly expresses his sentiments about Americans struggling for independence and control of the continent, warning that there is a spiritual conflict associated with the conduct of the war. Hammon was writing in the midst of very tumultuous times. He began publishing for the first time at the beginning of revolutionary activity in the colonies, and much of his writing occurred during the revolution itself, when the concepts of freedom, natural rights, and property were being codified in religious as well as secular terms. This period also saw slaves begin to question and openly revolt against their masters, as opportunities for emancipation arose under British occupation. The British openly recruited slaves in the southern colonies, promising emancipation after the war. In this atmosphere, the Lloyd family allowed Hammon, a loyal and trusted servant, to defend publicly the rights to property in human chattel even as the Lloyds fought for political independence.

Commentators generally fail to connect Hammon's subject matter and the timing of his poems and essays, which mark them as part of both the political and the religious discourse of the revolutionary period. Hammon's most obvious political statement addressing the exigencies of the time occurs in "A Dialogue Entitled the Kind Master and the Dutiful Servant," in which he wrote,

Servant
Dear Master Now it is a time,
   A time of great distress;
We'll follow after things divine,
   And pray for happiness.

Master
Then will happy a day appear.
   That virtue shall increase;
Lay up the sword and drop the spear,
   And Nations Seek for peace.[53]

This poem acknowledges the conflict between the colonies and Britain and expresses loyalty during a time of crisis that tested concepts of liberty. It represents a paternal relationship between servant and master and skirts the issue of perpetual servitude in the form of religious discourses formulated through the principles of an orthodox Calvinism that could account for most of the ambiguities between Christianity and the political activities of slave masters. The fact that he was a slave arguing for slavery's compatibility with Christian principles added further credibility to the idea that slavery was an institution of benevolent paternalism.

Many commentaries on Hammon's writing fall short by failing to examine the internal and intertextual consistency of Hammon's understanding of Christian doctrine throughout his works. Scholars usually explain *Christian* and *doctrine* in very vague terms, but getting at the sense of Hammon's writing requires that these matters be carefully outlined and brought into interpretations of his works. Specifically, while Hammon's writings exhibit the fundamentals of what could become a language of resistance to slavery, the specifics of his works nevertheless reveal an accommodation to slavery. Hammon says nothing about the perpetuation or abolition of slavery not voiced by antiabolitionists. For example, Hammon might approve of a gradualist approach to ending slavery, as he indicates in "An Address to the Negroes in the State of New York," but only insofar as masters may grant liberty to their slaves as a reward for good conduct.[54] He acknowledges an inconsistency between the conduct of masters during the Revolutionary War in seeking their liberty and the continued practice of slavery, further stating that "liberty is a great thing and worth seeking" but is also "by no means the greatest thing [slaves] have to be concerned about."[55] Hammon states early in his essay, "I am certain that while we are slaves, it is our duty to obey our masters, in all their lawful commands, and mind them unless we are bid to do that which we know to be sin, or forbidden in God's word. The apostle Paul says: Servants be obedient to them that are your masters according to the flesh, with fear and trembling in singleness in your heart as unto Christ . . . doing the will of God from the heart."[56] Hammon saw no inconsistency between the idea that slavery is a burden or "labour" to the enslaved and the idea that slavery is also a part of the will of God, not to be resisted. Slavery places on the enslaved the burden of "labours" for others that will eventually lead to salvation for slaves if they attend to their burdens as if doing them in the service of Christ, a lesson consistent with all of Hammon's writings. Masters bear the burden of being benevolent and paternalistic caretakers of their slaves, neither abusing nor neglecting them.

Although commentators have frequently cited "An Address to the Negroes in the State of New York" as evidence of Hammon's antislavery attitudes, the views concerning slavery actually found therein may acknowledge that liberty is worth seeking yet also that slavery is the will of God; abolition is therefore not to be an active goal unless it is bestowed in return for good behavior through the benevolence of the worldly masters to whom God has entrusted the slave.

Hammon's writings, particularly his poetry, have another aspect that deserves further attention: the way that the form of his works informs the content of his expressed ideas. The formal components of Hammon's work offer, as previous commentators have pointed out, a valuable starting point for examining the beginnings of the African American tradition of letters.[57] His poems generally followed the form of the folk ballad, which grew out of and developed into a spiritual tradition that enabled poor black people to remember and transmit the religious messages that sustained them.

Hammon's first published poem, "An Evening Thought, Salvation by Christ, with Penitential Cries," which appeared when he was forty-nine, helps to magnify what was most important to Hammon's understanding of Christianity, particularly Calvinist doctrines of total depravity and an emphasis on the necessity of Christ in attaining salvation. In this poem, Hammon constructs a poetic voice that operates within the ideology of Calvinist culture. "Salvation Comes by Christ alone / The only Son of God," declare the opening two lines of Hammon's poem, highlighting this central theme of his work and a central doctrine of orthodox Calvinist theology. This idea of the necessity of Christ for salvation and of selection appears no fewer than seventeen times in this eighty-eight-line poem. Its constant repetition probably reflects the type of Christian instruction that Hammon received throughout his life. This lesson emphasized the futility of worldly desires and efforts as well as the dream of and faith in a glorious afterlife.

When Hammon relates a more concrete verse on salvation, it takes the form of the Rapture to come at the end of time:

Salvation be thy leading Staff,
   To set the Sinner free.
Dear Jesus unto thee we fly;
   Depart, depart from Sin
Salvation doth at length supply,
   The glory of our King.[58]

The equation of freedom and Rapture also appears consistently in Hammon's later poems and was intended to be taken literally by the slaves who needed to reconcile the concepts of freedom and Christian belief with their condition as slaves.

The insistent repetition of doctrines of depravity and the abstractions of Christian love and salvation that appear in Hammon's poem conveniently allow slave owners to argue to their slaves that resistance and revolt are not consistent with freedom from their condition, that their "salvation" is spiritual, a salvation of the future open to those who follow Christ's teachings of love and obedience. For the "dark benighted Souls" of humans, "Salvation comes from God we know," and the duty of the sinner is to "love his holy Word."[59]

Hammon's poem is very abstract throughout, but it emphasizes a belief in human depravity and the necessity to wait patiently for Christ to be the actor in the salvation of mankind, a sentiment expressed more directly in "An Evening's Improvement," written in the spring of 1783: "Here my brethren we see that it is our indispensable duty to conform to the will of God in all things, not having our hearts set on the pleasures of this life; but we must prepare for death, our great and last change. For we are sinners by nature, and are adding thereunto by evil practices."[60] Hammon states that this sermon was written "for the advantage of my friends" and was encouraged "by my superiors" because of their admiration for his sound theology and advice. The "friends" were probably a congregation of slaves and other blacks, because it is very unlikely that Hammon would have been allowed to exhort a congregation of Hartford, Connecticut, elites. However, the pronouncement, "For we are sinners by nature, and are adding thereunto by evil practices," is a traditional expression of Calvinist views of human nature that would have been recognized and agreed to by a British-American congregation and readership of Calvinist leaning. Drawing from John 1:29, this sermon appeals to Christians to look to Christ "in the sense of the text, that is, in a spiritual" rather than literal manner.[61]

One of the major themes throughout Hammon's works is that the Scriptures are spiritual guides for how to live but do not condone any particular actions in which humans might engage. In fact, Hammon looks suspiciously at human activity, especially when these actions operate in the interests of attaining worldly comfort and ideals of justice. Since Calvinist theology holds that humans are "sinners by nature," they can do nothing that does not compound their sinfulness. There can also be no justice that is not in accordance with God's will, and God's will is knowable and reflected in the reality of the moment: "Thus, my dear brethren, we are to follow the lamb of God, at all times, whether in prosperity [or] adversity, knowing that all things work together for good, to them that love God."[62] Hammon was deeply embedded in Edwardian Calvinism and New Divinity that emphasized disinterested benevolence and the idea that God not only allows sin to exist in the world but actively wills it into existence for good ends. Slaves' condition, therefore, is the will of God, and slaves must be patient and content that in due time, reward for their long sufferings will come. To resist and fight for temporal freedom, in Hammon's theology, is to forget the Christian obligation to masters and God. Such a form of selfishness and self-love is sinful. Hammon believed that people should be willing to suffer the hardships of slavery for the greater glory of God.

Although Samuel Hopkins opposed slavery, his system of beliefs influenced Hammon's work and was adaptable to the service of slavery. It is no accident that Hammon's writing disdains human activity—the idea that worldly works could bring about freedom and salvation—and supports the contention that servants must serve their masters' interests even if the system under which they worked was sinful. Hammon wrote unequivocally in "An Address to the Negroes in the State of New York" that God "has commanded us to obey, and we ought to do this cheerfully, and freely. This should be done by us not only because God commands, but because our own peace and comfort depend on it."[63] Even if slavery is a sin, it is obviously the will of God that slaves be loyal to their masters. Doing so helps their own "peace and comfort," and if masters who keep slaves are "wicked in keeping us so, we cannot help it; they must answer to God for it."[64] This text marks the height of Hammon's theological development and lays out the terms under which slaves should be involved in the abolition of slavery—not at all. This belief in passive obedience is no simple declaration but rather the culmination of a system of belief that Hammon had adopted, preached, and practiced throughout his life. Hammon's complex system of orthodox Calvinist doctrine and New Divinity beliefs is visible throughout his works and gives insight into how many black Christians practiced in the context of difficult religious and political circumstances.

Nevertheless, Hammon lived in a time of great turmoil and change, and he ultimately came to believe that if slavery were to come to an end, abolition should come about gradually. Older slaves who had grown up in the system "have always had masters to take care of us, [and] should hardly know how to take care of ourselves"; "I should be glad if others, especially the young Negroes, were to be free."[65] These statements accord with many of the gradualist approaches to emancipation being debated at the time. Slaves were not believed to be ready for freedom or ready to participate in the democratic process as citizens, and many people believed that a careful, slow approach to emancipation must result. Younger slaves would be manumitted at twenty-one, after serving masters in preparation for their release. Hammon believed that a spirit of benevolence would or should eventually cause masters to free their slaves. But slaves had to prove their readiness for emancipation and "by our good conduct prevail on our masters to set us free."[66] Although Hammon expressed this political sentiment in religious terms here and in his poetry, many abolitionists throughout America echoed the idea, sincerely believing that gradual emancipation was the only practical way to prepare slaves for participation in British-American culture.

According to Oscar Wegelin, who in the early 1970s recovered and commented on Hammons's poetry, "It seems . . . too bad that his verse is entirely of a religious nature. Much would be added to its interest had he written about some of the events that were transpiring all around him during the War for Independence and the years that followed that struggle."[67] This lament has remained prevalent in criticism of early black writers. Their work and ideas have often been judged as inferior or unimportant precisely because they were expressed in a religious idiom. Eighteenth-century society did not separate religion and politics into distinctly different categories, as is the case today. In fact, writers would have been expected to express and defend their political views by connecting them to Christian principles. Thus, Hammon and many other black writers of the period can in fact reveal quite a bit about the political events of the time through their religious discourses.

Black people—particularly slaves—living in eighteenth-century British America had only limited means for expressing themselves. The literacy rate was very low among the free black population, and in many places, laws forbade slaves from learning to read or write. However, song was one means of expression and communication among slaves that was allowed and even encouraged, especially as growing numbers of black Christian converts began meeting together and remaking European hymns to express an understanding and vision of spirituality suited to slaves' particular circumstances and conditions in the New World.[68] Slaves developed the spiritual, which British-American masters saw as pure entertainment, to communicate ideas and information both within small groups and across long distances. These songs expressed the slaves' identification and interpretations of the Bible within the light of their experiences, including interactions with their masters, their current social milieu, and the received culture of African peoples passed down across generations.[69]

The spiritual tradition developed primarily in the fields and other places of extreme repetitive labor, and Hammon sought to bring a Christian message to his people through this creative medium. His poetry may have been written and published in broadsides for a British-American audience, but its form also reveals the influence of traditional oral learning. His poems doubled as religious odes structured to be sung as well as read. These writings reveal a sophisticated knowledge of meter and rhyme usually associated with traditional folk ballads. His poems could be sung as hymns, and his use of iambic trochees and alliteration attests to a form that could be easily memorized and repeated. As one of the few literate blacks among a group of Christianized slaves, Hammon would have been a leader, and he wrote hymns according to folk traditions that would aid his fellow slaves in memorizing and expressing the Christian principles important to their spiritual growth and survival. Hammon did not create or pioneer an oral tradition, but European hymnody combined with his background and submersion in a primarily oral African American culture led him to adopt and innovate within a tradition that was developing into a vibrant new form of American spiritual music. He made his works and religious ideals accessible and transmittable to and by other African Americans, most of them illiterate but with similar interests in religious thinking and expression through language.

Another look at "An Evening Thought" reveals the careful way in which Hammon crafted this poem to readily be sung as well as read. The poem can be divided into twenty-two coherent stanzas, with the lines of each stanza an alternating sequence of iambic trochee—a stressed syllable followed by an unstressed syllable. The first and third lines are four metrical feet in length (tetrametric), and the second and fourth lines consist of three metrical feet (trimeter):

> Salvation comes by Jesus Christ alone,
> > The only Son of God;
> Redemption now to every one,
> > That loves his holy Word.[70]

This meter is fairly consistent throughout the poem. Although the first line has five feet, it is the only one that breaks the pattern of tetrametric lines. An occasional departure from meter is common in folk ballads. However, the alternating tetrameters and trimeters within each stanza form the traditional ballad stanza of oral folk tradition.

Further connecting the poem to an oral tradition of verse, Hammon uses alliteration and assonance rather than depending on end rhymes. The poem's end-rhyme scheme is inconsistent and mainly composed of approximate rhymes, a pattern that is also consistent with the folk ballad form:

Salvation be thy leading Staff,
　To Set the Sinner free.
Dear Jesus unto thee we fly;
　Depart, depart from Sin
Salvation doth at length supply,
　The glory of our King.[71]

The repetition of the *s* sound in this section of the poem illustrates his use of alliteration and consonance as mnemonic devices, as does the repetition of the long and short *e* in every line except "The glory of our king," which uses the repetition of long and short *o*. These devices run throughout this poem and are major features of all Hammon's known poetry.

Hammon's aesthetic is no accident. He undoubtedly learned his forms over many years, and they make the poem's ideas accessible to the singer or listener. Alliteration, consonance, and assonance aid memory, as does the repetition of certain key words. Hammon frequently uses *salvation*, *glory*, and *redemption* in this poem. These words may serve as place markers, but they also represent an ideal that marries form with content. Some commentators have suggested that Hammon's use of repeating words and phrases is a mark of his limited learning. On the contrary, however, this repetition indicates his deep and thorough knowledge of biblical verse structure and the importance of structure to meaning and interpretation. As Albert Raboteau has written in his landmark *Slave Religion: The "Invisible Institution" in the Antebellum South*, slaves' singing style, "which was influenced by their African heritage, was characterized by a strong emphasis on call and response, polyrhythms, syncopation, ornamentation, slides from one note to another, and repetition."[72] Hammon's poems clearly represent many of these qualities, pointing to the influence of African traditions on the aesthetic styles he combined to form his unique poetry.

Form and content are strongly interrelated and inseparable. Repetition of concepts and ideas parallels the syntactic structures of biblical texts, operating to emphasize important and recurring themes essential to the underlying belief system. The system of belief and the system of representation through language thus correspond with one another and become recognizable ideological constructions within certain discourse communities. In the text's overall meaning, the physical use of repetition—particularly of certain words or sounds—carries cultural significance equal to that of the individual words or utterances.

In a primarily oral society, structure connects words and their semiotic value to other lived experiences. Hammon was therefore tying the biblical structures of words to the primarily oral traditions of his black audience.

Hammon is a troubling figure in any discussion of evangelism and resistance. He was, without a doubt, a very accommodating individual with regard to slavery. Many scholars have attempted to defend him as a model of resistance, but these studies seem to be more hopeful than convincing, particularly in light of the evidence Hammon left behind. For the purposes of this book, Hammon exemplifies the way in which black evangelicals adopted and used abstract principles and theologies of traditional European Christian practice to inform their worldviews and politics. Hammon did not, would not, and perhaps could not for any number of reasons advance a Christianity with a radical politic. His work shows, however, that African peoples were beginning to develop complex theological principles and politics that grew out of traditional forms of Christianity. These ideals found print at a crucial and querulous time when many of the orthodox beliefs Hammon advocated were being called into question. Apparent accommodation notwithstanding, Hammon engaged in the general religious and political print discourse of his time and contributed to the spread of Christianity among black people in his region, allowing and even forcing others to begin systematizing an alternative set of Christian principles for the purposes of resistance. Hammon is far from a socially dead piece of property: his prose and poetry expresses an identification with a society and an active engagement in the intellectual and political concerns of the time. And abolitionists used the fact that Hammon could and did engage his readers with a sophisticated knowledge and expression of religious principle to prove black humanity and merit, thereby supporting emancipatory politics.

Although, as Orlando Patterson has shown, socialized death is an imperative in maintaining the order of a slaveholding society, African peoples living in the colonies increasingly began to think of themselves as a distinct social group with a common destiny. Hammon's system of belief maintained a common human identification through Christ and a destiny that was connected to the end of time, when the elect would be lifted into the Kingdom of God. But Hammon's writings do not provide evidence of resistance to slavery; for that, readers must look to one of his contemporaries, Phillis Wheatley, the first black slave writer who strongly and consistently spoke against the institution of slavery, using her work to gain her independence and freedom.

CHAPTER TWO

Phillis Wheatley and the Charge toward Progressive Black Theologies

In May 1773, a young woman named Phillis Wheatley boarded a merchant ship named the *London Packet* that was sailing from Boston to London. Several Boston newspapers announced her journey, noting that she was being escorted by the wealthy owner of the ship and celebrating the young woman as an "extraordinary" poet of "ingenious" capacity.[1] Such announcements of the comings and goings of ships and their prominent passengers were common practice, information of interest to the publications' general readers. But the notices regarding Wheatley were remarkable because the woman who would soon be hailed internationally as a poet was also a slave.

The African-born Wheatley had already completed one transatlantic voyage aboard a merchant ship, but her first crossing had started on the west coast of Africa, most likely from the Senegambia region, and ended on the American continent, where she was sold as property. The *Boston Evening Post* had also reported that arrival, in 1761: "TO BE SOLD. A parcel of Likely NEGROES, imported from Africa, cheap for Cash."[2] Just six years after being captured, Wheatley had mastered the English language, so precocious that by age twelve or thirteen she was already writing poetry that not only constituted interesting verse but also criticized slavery as against nature and God. Her works hailed the ideals of liberty that British North Americans were adopting as a philosophical basis for organizing government and society. Although temporally separated from her land of origin, family, and language, Wheatley quickly connected to a new language and constructed an identity that was both self-consciously African and African American.

Wheatley identified strongly with both her identities by means of a theology that allowed her the intellectual, psychological, and literary liberation necessary to lead to her physical emancipation from human bondage. Although a slave, Wheatley realized the potential of language and religion to bring into existence a social reality of liberation for African peoples in British North America. She therefore involved herself in the literary and political discourses of the time. Her efforts to write herself into the cultural and political conversations of the period culminated in the publication of a book of poetry, *Poems on Various Subjects, Religious and Moral,* that gained Wheatley further access and recognition in revolutionary-era international discussions concerning the nature of liberty and liberation. Wheatley's poetry brings together varying fields of knowledge under the sphere of theology to place her works within the intellectual tradition of late-eighteenth-century evangelicalism, a burgeoning and increasingly intellectual tradition that involved the integration of classical learning and contemporary philosophy and theology into social practice. As a result of this work as a poet and cultural ambassador, Wheatley became a controversial figure, the subject of discussion from the American revolutionary period to the present.

Contemporary scholars and critics have rediscovered the significance of Wheatley, principally through the works of William H. Robinson, Sondra O'Neale, John Shields, Mukhtar Ali Isani, and James A. Levernier.[3] During the 1970s and 1980s, she was periodically excoriated for such alleged personal transgressions as being "taught by Whites to think white" or writing "very few poems in which [she] points to her experiences as a Black and a slave." She was even dubbed spiritually "mutilated."[4] These charges are at best misguided and are usually informed by selective readings of particular texts or by a misunderstanding of eighteenth-century history and culture.[5] Many of the negative attacks on Wheatley's poetry amount to little more than proof-texting that arrives at conclusions at odds with the content of the larger body of her existing works. Nevertheless, some scholars and educators have accepted and repeated these accusations, probably in part because legitimate political concerns regarding race and representation in the arts and education as the Black Arts and Black Power movements worked to reform America's racial politics. Many of the scholars engaged in this effort have not perceived Wheatley as exhibiting an aesthetic that conformed to mid-twentieth-century efforts to abolish institutionalized forms of prejudice and bigotry.[6] More sensitive and less polemical evaluations would have revealed, as O'Neale has, that Wheatley used her poetry to challenge the traditional Western biblical typology of "antagonistic black and white color imagery."[7] Prominent critics commented negatively on Wheatley's works during her own time as well: Thomas Jefferson, for example, dismissed her writing precisely because it was at odds with ideas about the racial inferiority of African peoples and because it threatened the slavery establishment. Across these three centuries, the racial issues have remained connected, although they have changed in degree and kind. Wheatley's principal concern was spreading a philosophy of universal equality and human rights through Christian evangelism, which she saw as the means to freedom for the oppressed.

Wheatley's brilliance combined with her social/legal status as a slave forced the defenders and beneficiaries of human bondage to rethink arguments supporting slavery based on innate inferiority of Africans or to resort to claiming that Wheatley and numerous other blacks like her were mere exceptions. A third option was to dismiss her work out of hand as inferior, as Jefferson did in *Notes on the State of Virginia* (1785).[8] However, positive evaluations of Wheatley's writings by such powerful English political figures as Selina Hastings (the Countess of Huntingdon) and Granville Sharp as well as highly respected Americans including Benjamin Rush and Benjamin Franklin meant that Wheatley could not simply be ignored. (Franklin paid Wheatley a visit in 1773, prior to the publication of her book of poetry.) Wheatley's renown as a poet and her skill as a cultural ambassador led her to exchange letters with George Washington, and she spent a half hour visiting with him not long after his appointment as commander in chief of the Continental Army.[9] Out of either vanity or sincere patronage, Washington had Wheatley's poem to him published in the *Virginia Gazette*: it appeared on page 1 on March 20, 1776, and made Wheatley undeniably a writer for the revolutionary cause.[10]

Nevertheless, others continued to see Wheatley and her writing as a threat to preconceived notions about Africans and the legitimacy of slavery. By the time Jefferson attacked her work, she had already died and could not defend herself, but her writing had nevertheless significantly affected transatlantic culture, and her record of association with the American cause and many of its founders vindicated her status both as a poet and as an intellectual interested in involvement in the American Revolution, which she associated with the larger goal of universal freedom and an end to slavery. Still, much scholarship has focused very narrowly on her explicit attitudes toward race and slavery, on the obvious moments when she speaks out against bigotry and slavery, rather than examining the nuances of her writing and thought.[11] As Katherine Clay Bassard has pointed out, such narrow views of what constitutes an "authentic" black text have hampered "attempts to articulate a vernacular theory for creating narratives of African American literary tradition" and "threatened to exclude the plethora of texts . . . being rescued from the archives."[12]

Although Wheatley has consistently been quoted and anthologized since the publication of her book of poems, her work has generally been overlooked for what it can offer readers concerning history, ethics, aesthetics, theology, and other areas of inquiry; it has been examined only as an artifact of racial representation. Her book and other extant writings fall into two intellectual traditions, the American tradition and the African American tradition of ideals and letters. Two overriding philosophies guided Wheatley's thought: Enlightenment philosophy and revolutionary theology.

Wheatley was in every respect a product of the Enlightenment and its contradictions. In addition to writing poetry that found syncretism between Christianity and the classical tradition, Wheatley was thoroughly interested in Enlightenment philosophy and often found ways to integrate her interests and knowledge of scientific principles with Christian ideals. One poem that illustrates Wheatley's translation of scientific principles into Christian thought is "Thoughts on the Works of Providence." Generally read as a purely evangelical and pious meditation, this selection constitutes the third-longest piece in *Poems on Various Subjects*; its 132 lines trail only "Niobe in Distress" (224 lines) and "Goliath of Gath" (222 lines), both of which were epyllia, or short epics.[13] Although "Thoughts on the Works of Providence" does not qualify as an epyllion, it is an evangelical piece that integrates a praise poem on the nature of God with a scientific explanation of his role as "first cause" in the creation and sustenance of the universe. God is the "monarch of the earth, and skies," and Wheatley casts him as the architect and mover of the universe.[14] Wheatley easily and comfortably integrates evangelical language with that of science, acknowledging the majesty of creation by an omnipotent God as well as scientific explanations of the cosmos. In this poem, Wheatley uses Newtonian characterizations of the universe as a "vast machine" to explain God as a creator and maintainer of its mechanisms. The sun is the center of this "machine":

> Though to his eye its mass a point appears:
> Ador'd the God that whirls surrounding spheres.
> Which first ordain'd that mighty *Sol* should reign
> The peerless monarch of th' ethereal train
> Of miles twice forty millions is his height,
> and yet his radiance dazzles mortal sight.[15]

Wheatley imagines the relative sizes of God, the sun, the earth, and its inhabitants, with God observing the sun as but a mere point while humanity is dazzled by the radiance of the sun though it is "of miles twice forty millions" distant from the earth. But Wheatley does not merely compare relative sizes; she enthralls readers with a sense of awe at the grandeur of both creation and God's existence in relation to it. Wheatley's description evokes a sense of the sublime in readers' imaginations as they picture the vast discrepancy between the perceptions of humans and that of God. In her own way, she creatively begins the process of explaining God's sovereignty, first by scale and then by moving on to divine will:

> That *Wisdom*, which attends *Jehovah's* ways,
> Shines most conspicuous in the solar rays:

Without them, destitute of heat and light,
This world would be the reign of endless night.[16]

The wisdom of God, the divine will, makes for a sun that sustains humans' comfortable environment on the planet. Further praising God for the sun and the "beauteous dies, / that spread through all the circuit of the skies," Wheatley also illustrates her adoration of God as the first cause of all that she holds dear.[17] Wheatley's use of eighteenth-century scientific and mathematical terminology throughout this poem to describe God and his relation to the "circuit of the skies" shows her skill with not only classical allusion but also the language of science. In using such words and phrases as *mass, point, spheres, solar rays,* and *circuit of the skies* while characterizing God as first cause of all these principles and their harmonious relation to one another, Wheatley depicts God's sovereignty over the universe and its movements. For Wheatley, the language of science was just as useful for describing humanity's relationship to God as for describing the universe's seemingly mechanistic workings.

Wheatley also uses the language of science to express a relationship between humanity and God in "To the University of Cambridge in New England," another evangelical poem published in *Poems on Various Subjects.* The first and final stanzas of this poem are usually cited as examples of Wheatley's consciousness (or lack thereof) concerning her African origins. However, commentators rarely mention that this poem urges educated students to remember their duty to God. The poem also acknowledges the seemingly secular duty of its audience:

Students, to you 'tis giv'n to scan the heights
Above, to traverse the ethereal space,
And mark the systems of revolving worlds.[18]

For university students, these are legitimate and crucial parts of an education, and Wheatley uses her knowledge of the curriculum as a segue into the more important recognition of redemption:

Still more, ye sons of science ye receive
The blissful news by messengers from heav'n
How *Jesus'* blood for your redemption flows.[19]

Using scientific language and recognizing students as "sons of science" provides Wheatley a useful metaphor that plays off of vision and the action of looking into the sky: just as the students "scan the heights," "traverse the ethereal space," and "mark systems of revolving worlds," they must also collect from the heavens the "blissful news" of redemption. The sky or the heavens is the domain of God, home to the messages of creation and redemption as well as the findings of astronomy. Wheatley recognizes this parallel role of the skies and uses the languages of both astronomy and evangelism to show her belief in the mutual ability of science and religion to reveal universal truths. The "messengers from heav'n" to whom the poem refers are ambiguous but may refer either to the positions and motions of celestial bodies, which Wheatley believes reveal God's wisdom and sovereignty, "Thoughts on the Works of Providence" demonstrates, or to the Gospels, the "good news" that Wheatley would have recognized as divinely inspired works.[20] Wheatley believes that God's presence and plans are encoded in both the sky and the Bible. Wheatley's faith in science's compatibility with religion was neither unusual nor incompatible with Enlightenment philosophy, as scientific and mathematical visionaries of the period also believed that the enlightened age would reveal the presence of God's influence in the creation and maintenance of the universe.[21]

Two of the four specifically evangelical poems that appear in *Poems on Various Subjects* use scientific and mathematical terminology to impart information or descriptions about divinity or humanity's relationship to God.[22] These poems demonstrate that Wheatley did not hesitate to relate what are often thought of as varying fields of knowledge to religion and piety. Therein lies part of the timeliness of Wheatley's poetry in general and of *Poems on Various Subjects* in particular. Wheatley, like many of her American and British contemporaries who also worked to understand the relationships among various fields of knowledge, reconciles Enlightenment intellectualism and classical learning with her knowledge of theology.[23] Wheatley's decision to self-consciously integrate various fields of knowledge into her poetry lends it an impressive depth and variety. Her efforts to bring together science and classicism under the sphere of theology place her squarely within the intellectual tradition of late-eighteenth-century evangelists, who also took seriously classical learning and its integration into contemporary philosophy and social practice.[24]

Wheatley's slave status and African heritage stood in the way of her goal of expressing a serious intellectual poetry of evangelical ethics in a British-American context. Her status as a slave seems at odds with the period's humanistic tendencies but nonetheless formed part of it. Wheatley was fully conscious of this problem and worked both in her writing and her actions to confront the biases against her and her poetry. But by the time she was ready to publish a collection of her poetry in 1772, she needed someone to attest to the authenticity of her writing. Prominent members of Massachusetts's government and elite society tested her knowledge and skills to prove that her works were indeed her own.[25] But even such authentication could not secure her a publishing deal in North America.

By this time, Wheatley was known to be an American slave of African origin, but she also emphasized her identity as an African in her poetry while espousing a belief in the revolutionary movement taking place in British North America, a fact that would not be lost on those sensitive to proslavery factions. Publishing the works of an African slave who was clearly intelligent and creative and who articulated the principles of liberation and universal humanity posed too big a threat to the institution of slavery, since her skills debunked many of the rationales for perpetuation the practice of slavery. In short, Wheatley and her poetry were far too political. The testimonials to her ability likely worked against her, and her goal of publishing a collection of poems with explicitly pro-American and anti-British themes would have to take a back seat to a carefully reworked collection that would sell overseas, in the British market.

Although the collection maintained a pro-American tenor, it was also much more conciliatory toward British political sensibilities. Wheatley included twenty-three completely new poems not mentioned in the original 1772 proposal and likely written between February 1772 and July 1773.[26] Wheatley appears to have transformed her book so that she could spread her vision of social reality and piety through her art.[27] Part of that social reality involved burgeoning attitudes about the nature of race and universal humanity and the relationships between the peoples of Africa and Europe, topics that had already directly influenced events in her life.

Certainly by 1772 and likely long before, Wheatley realized an important connection between religion and civil government. She remarked in one letter that "chaos, which has reigned so long, is converting into beautiful Order, and reveals more and more clearly, the glorious Dispensation of civil and religious Liberty, which are so inseparably united, that there is little or no Enjoyment of the one without the other."[28] Even without the testimony of this letter to the Reverend Samson Occom, the style and content of Wheatley's poetry clearly show that she had come to this conclusion about the connection between civil engagement and religious thought. She believes that one must not abandon civic engagement for a passive hopefulness that God alone will bring about positive change in the social order. God plays a role in the affairs of humanity and is, in Wheatley's theology, a first cause, as is illustrated in "To the University of Cambridge in New England" and "Thoughts on the Works of Providence." But what Wheatley describes as "virtue" ultimately is those actions undertaken by individuals in the spirit of accomplishing the desires of the divine order on earth. "On Virtue," the second poem in the 1773 collection, defines the relationship of virtue to intellect, soul, and temporal time. She realizes that the effort to know virtue in a purely intellectual sense is in vain and declares, "I cease to wonder, and no more attempt / Thine height t' explore, or fathom thy profound." An apparently transcendent concept such as virtue lies beyond the capacity for human understanding and cannot be known as a purely intellectual concept. But failure in the effort to know virtue as a concept does not preclude virtue from lying within the human soul's grasp. The human soul is capable of what the mind or intellect is not. Although "wisdom is higher than the fool can reach," the soul, in contrast, should "sink not into despair, / *Virtue* is near thee, hovers over thine head." Although virtue cannot be counted in intellectual terms, the human "heav'n-born" soul clearly can access it, and in Calvinist thinking, the soul animates the human being; the soul is the breath of life. The human soul and virtue are therefore closely aligned not as thought but as action: "O leave me not to the false joys of time! / But guide my steps to endless life and bliss." Wheatley seeks heaven but realizes that the animate soul must be guided by virtue toward the accomplishment of a temporal life worthy of bliss in an eternal afterlife. These ideas about the nature of the human soul and what constitutes true virtue lie at the heart of Wheatley's theology, which insists that humanity is responsible for making manifest its salvation through virtuous activity, with an emphasis on divine love rather than the impulse toward fear of the irascible God of orthodox Calvinism.[29] This theological perspective also contributes to Wheatley's further attitudes toward politics. If social justice is to be obtained, it must come through the actions of human agents working toward the wishes and ultimate design of God, with an eye toward benevolence rather than forced attrition.

Wheatley not only recognized the usefulness of Christian discourse for discussing and organizing political circumstances; she also believed that Christianity was the way to model behavior in an independent and free nation. Wheatley was an unusual patriot—a woman, an African, and a slave whose primary support for her book came from the same nation, Great Britain, that she often criticized in her writing for its imperial excesses. Her status as a slave also resulted from the laws and practices of the same nation she wanted to see liberated from foreign pressures. But Wheatley sees the political liberation of the colonies as a step toward universal liberation, as a part of the unfolding of biblical history, with the chaos of an older, sinful world transforming into one of preordained order.

Scholars have argued that Wheatley wrote many "subversive" poems criticizing slavery. More accurately, however, eighteenth-century readers would have perceived most of Wheatley's poems that discuss slavery as opposing the institution. But her poems directly criticizing Great Britain are more subversive. Several of the works in *Poems on Various Subjects* appear on the surface to be purely evangelical but actually offer highly political commentaries on the nature of empire and power, especially as it affects the relationship between America and Great Britain. Wheatley portrays a set of political positions based on her modern concepts of North America's place in the international milieu and the significance of slavery as a sin.

By the time Wheatley was ready to publish her *Poems on Various Subjects*, political ties between British North America and England were becoming increasingly strained. One of Wheatley's most interesting political poems masquerading as a purely evangelical verse is her "Isaiah lxiii. 1–8," one of six political poems in the book. Although Wheatley chose not to include her more damning poems about England, "Isaiah lxiii. 1–8" offers a more measured warning of God's divine predilection toward the Americans than "On the Affray in King-Street, on the Evening of the 5th of March," "To Samuel Quincey, Esq.; *a Panegyrick*," or "On America," all of which were omitted. The biblical book of Isaiah is a message of judgment on Judah (Israel), predicting that God's wrath as a consequence of bad behavior would subject the nation to punishments but further foreseeing that Israel ultimately will be preserved through God's salvation of those who return to him. Although God expresses great wrath, Isaiah's message ends as one of hope.[30] Part of Isaiah's inspiration for this message was the encroaching Assyrian empire, which eventually absorbed Judah and subjected the Hebrew people to foreign rule for the next several centuries. The book of Isaiah thus reflects the Hebrew people's anxiety regarding their nation's future and the prospect of living under foreign rule.

Wheatley's retelling of a small section of Isaiah is a multilayered rephrasing of the story that transposes the old Hebrew anxiety of "foreign" rule on the American situation with Great Britain from a predestinarian, Christian nationalist perspective, where the voice of God and that of Christ are one, transcending time to address simultaneously both the past and the future. The verse pits of the small but defiant nation of Israel against the far more powerful Assyria, which wreaks great havoc on the smaller nation but does not quite conquer it. Wheatley combines Old Testament apocalypse of national ruin with New Testament fulfillment of God's promise of salvation and the creation of a Zion—in this case, an American Zion.

> Against thy *Zion* though her foes may rage,
> And all their cunning, all their strength engage,
> Yet she serenely on thy bosom lies,
> Smiles at their arts, and all their force defies.[31]

In the context of British-American politics, this poem about the relationship between nations both placed contemporary politics within a biblical narrative and warned against armed conflict. But conflict was inevitable in Isaiah because of the sins of the chosen people, just as the revolutionary conflict was inevitable as a consequence of the sin of American slavery practiced by what Wheatley envisioned as God's chosen nation. Wheatley's comparison is apt, and although it is more overtly critical of the British than of the Americans, she nevertheless implies that even the chosen people are not without the stain of sin and that war is a product of God's divine justice in response to slavery as much as a result of British imperial malice. This is as close as Wheatley's poetry ever comes to a jeremiad, but the theme and structure of this particular poem allude to that tradition of biblical writing that both acknowledges a chosen people and scolds them for their transgressions.

Wheatley had to remove from her book the more overtly critical poems about the American situation, but she substituted poems such as "Isaiah lxiii. 1–8" that either warn against the catastrophic results of armed conflict between nations or praise England and its subjects for their pro-American policies and reversals of those policies Americans thought unfair. Although "Isaiah lxiii. 1–8" warns against the folly of fighting a nation in God's favor, other poems praise England. "To the King's Most Excellent Majesty. 1768," written when Wheatley was about fifteen years old, praises George III for the repeal of the 1765 Stamp Act. However, the poem still represents a discourse on the nature of power and the relationship between a ruler and the ruled, with an emphasis on peace and love rather than fear, conflict, and war.

> But how shall we the *British* king reward!
> Rule thou in peace, our father, and our lord!
> Midst the remembrance of thy favours past,
> The meanest peasants most admire the last. [32]

Peace through understanding on civil issues will allow the American colonies to "reward" King George III with allegiance. Wheatley lauds the king's repeal of the Stamp Act, writing that a "monarch's smile can set his subjects free." But this smile is guided by the dictates of a kind and benevolent God, and "freedom" is a quality that is both universal and ephemeral, depending on the actions and whims of God and humanity. Among humans, between king and subjects, a tension appears in this poem because the peace arrived at is negotiated, as the divine right of the king comes into question when it is at odds with the citizenry. Wheatley's view of governance includes no divine right of monarchies. Though she asks that "Great God, direct, and guard him from on high / and from his head let ev'ry evil fly!" the king has an obligation to the citizenry that she hopes will lead to peace and reward. Wheatley acknowledges George III's position as king and sovereign ruler of "num'rous nations," but the liberal philosophies of the time prevent her from assigning him or any other individual human supreme power over others. [33]

The book contains clear, explicit critiques of slavery, pointing to Wheatley's status in bondage. She does not hide her contempt for oppression in these poems—most obviously in "To the Right Honorable WILLIAM, Earl of Dartmouth" and "On Being Brought from AFRICA to AMERICA." But an underlying current in all of these poems critiquing the British Empire and Britain's relationship to America was also an attack on slavery, as the theme of universal humanity and rights runs throughout the book. This focus is evidenced by the repeated use of a positive theological system emphasizing the benevolent God of love over the irascible spirit of an older Calvinist tradition.

Wheatley's integration of a positive Calvinist theology that emphasizes the love of a sovereign God is at odds with her contemporaries' more negative and generally millennialist emphasis on divine wrath. Although Wheatley contemplates the significance of corporeal death and God's role as ruler of the universe, she does not dwell on death as punishment, wrath, or sign of impending apocalypse. The meaning of death nevertheless constitutes an important part of her writing. Phillis Wheatley and Jupiter Hammon share death as a recurring theme in their writings, always exploring its meaning within a Christian context. Whereas many Calvinist writers emphasized death as a terror, something dreadful described in generally negative terms, Wheatley took a very different perspective. Like Hammon, she wrote extensively on the subject, but it was less a dread occurrence than a release from the mortal world for a better state of existence in a heavenly paradise. Wheatley wrote negatively of death in only one poem, "To a Lady on the Death of Three Relations," but even that poem ends on a positive tone. The thirty-nine works in *Poems on Various Subjects* include fourteen eulogies, all of them composed in a standard form. "To a Lady and Her Children, on the Death of Her Son and Their Brother," best illustrates the structure of Wheatley's eulogies as well as her attitudes toward death.

With few variations, the structure of Wheatley eulogies falls into four parts. The first is the announcement of an occasion to mourn, such as when she states, "Oerwhelming sorrow now demands my song: / From death the overwhelming sorrow sprung."[34] The second part of the Wheatley eulogy is a description of the mourner's feelings of grief: "The brother weeps, the hapless sisters join / Th' increasing woe, and swell the crystal brine."[35] Third, Wheatley announces that the deceased has ascended into a higher state of being, into an otherworldly paradise to be forevermore enjoyed:

He, upon pinions swifter than the wind,
Has left mortality's sad scenes behind
For joys to this terrestrial state unknown,
And glories richer than the monarch's crown.[36]

Finally, the fourth section of a Wheatley eulogy instructs and sometimes scolds mourners not to belabor the passing of their loved one but to rejoice in his or her ascendance into a heavenly realm:

No more in briny show'rs, ye friends around,
Or bathe this clay, or waste them on the ground:
Still do you weep, still wish you his return?
How cruel thus to wish, and thus to mourn?[37]

Wheatley ends the final section on a high note, emphasizing the comforts of
the spiritual realm the deceased is to enjoy or celebrating the character of her
subject. The only exception to this structure occurs in "On the Death of the
Rev. Dr. SEWELL," which is more a praise poem celebrating an individual than
her usually structured eulogy. The other thirteen eulogies follow a general pattern, sometimes rearranging sections, lengthening and shortening them, but
always including the same four parts and always emphasizing the deceased's
ascendance to a heavenly paradise.

Wheatley's attitudes toward death suggest a radically different perspective
from Hammon's views regarding God, emphasizing grace and mercy over anger
and wrath. But further differences exist between Wheatley's and Hammon's
theological viewpoints. Unlike Wheatley, Hammon neither had nor sought to
integrate into his beliefs bold and sophisticated knowledge of civic duty or
revolutionary ideology. Although both evangelical writers were enslaved from
early childhood (with Hammon born into slavery in 1711 and Wheatley abducted around the age of five and transported to British North America) and
both received access to a degree of learning and comfort unusual for American slaves, only Wheatley understood and commented on the contradictions
between British-American revolutionary arguments regarding "natural rights"
and calls for liberty and the continuation of perpetual servitude on the American continent. Although Wheatley and Hammon shared slave status in British
America and although both were evangelical writers who expressed their ideas
in verse, they had very different views about the role of Africans and African-
descended people in determining their collective destinies on the continent.
Wheatley was much more outspoken and even aggressive in denouncing enslavement and oppression in her poetry and letters. She clearly condemned
slavery and bigotry, prompting Hammon's 1778 "An Address to Miss Phillis
Wheatley," giving her what he probably imagined was gentle encouragement to
focus more on God and less on politics. Wheatley did not advance a politics
of accommodation but wrote against Hammon's claims for slavery's religious
legitimacy. She thought and wrote about the promises of a liberal society that
included African-descended people. In a letter to the influential evangelical
Samuel Hopkins, Wheatley wrote, "Methinks Rev'd Sir, this is the beginning
of that happy period foretold by the prophets, when all shall know the Lord
from the least to the greatest." Whereas Hammon looked to a distant future on

the other side of death, Wheatley genuinely believed that humans should live for the moment and that humanity's efforts constituted a part of God's plan. Wheatley's statements about liberty and the impending Kingdom of Heaven on earth show that, like her contemporary, Hammon, she participated actively in the discussions regarding freedom, slavery, and religion, although the two slave poets were at odds about just how much participation God warranted. Hammon saw heaven as a future time to come after death; Wheatley saw it as impending and achievable through the activities of human agents working toward God's plan for a Zion. Wheatley recognized that religion and politics were not mutually exclusive. In fact, she could not speak "of one without the other" if she was to have any influence through the print media.[38] However, her positions on the issues of the time, influenced by a more liberal Calvinist doctrine, differed substantially from those of Hammon. He focused on the individual relationship with God and did not infuse a political awareness or civil duty into his religion. Wheatley, in contrast, envisioned a collective identity as an African and a much timelier destiny of freedom for enslaved Africans in liberal Christian society.

Although Wheatley, like Hammon, occupied a very tenuous position in her society, she nevertheless interacted and corresponded with people of influence who had similar interests. Her published letter to Occom is one illustration of her political interests and connections, but she also corresponded with John Thornton, Samuel Hopkins, and Thomas Woolridge, all of whom wielded great political and evangelical influence. Wheatley was also familiar with antislavery ministers such as Charles Chauncy, Samuel Cook, Samuel Sewell, and Samuel Cooper, all of whom lived in Boston and spoke out against slavery and the contradictions of elite Bostonian revolutionaries who cried out for liberty from the British but continued to hold African peoples in bondage.[39] Bassard has traced Wheatley's more emphatic statements against slavery in later revisions of her poems to the timing of her 1771 baptism at Boston's Old South Meeting House, a church whose ministers opposed slavery.[40]

Wheatley's connection to the Countess of Huntingdon, who became interested in the poet's career after she wrote a poem about the countess's personal chaplain, George Whitefield, is well known. The countess's influence likely led to Wheatley's first London publication, a eulogy to Whitefield that appeared at the end of a funeral sermon by Ebenezer Pemberton sold at Whitefield's Tabernacle Chapel in 1771.[41] The countess also sponsored the publication of *Poems on Various Subjects*. During Wheatley's 1773 visit to London to have an audience with her patron, Granville Sharp escorted the poet on a tour of the city. Given her status as a slave, Wheatley operated under many of the same constraints that Hammon probably faced. Nevertheless, her radical secularism led her activities and writing to express a self-awareness and sense of duty to her society and other Africans that Hammon lacked.

Although some contemporary critics have criticized Wheatley's work for being overly religious and not political enough, the middle-aged Hammon seemed to believe the opposite, warning Wheatley to seek heaven rather than meddle in earthly affairs.[42] Hammon would have read Wheatley's book of poetry and noticed the political tone and laments of many of its passages. By the time of the publication of his "Address to the Negroes of the State of New York," the revolution would have been in full swing, and he advised Wheatley to stay out of the way of the revolutionaries and the cause for which they fought, believing that her destiny, like that of other slaves, including himself, was heavenly:

> The Humble soul shall fly to God
>> And leave the things of time,
> Start forth as 'twere at the first word,
>> To taste things more divine.[43]

Wheatley's writing, however, remained as political as it was religious. Although Hammon was aware of her and wrote a poem to her, and although Wheatley counted herself one within a tradition of African artists and writers such as the poet Terrence and the African painter she addressed in "To S.M. a Young *African* Painter, on Seeing His Works," her writings never mention Hammon or his works. Though evangelical and concerned with the souls of humanity, Wheatley was also distinctly political, and by 1778 she likely found calls for silence and accommodation anathema to her mission as a revolutionary African American Christian writer—that is, to see her nation delivered from British control as part of God's unfolding plan for universal freedom for all humanity.

After her manumission, Wheatley began to generate more overtly political pieces supporting the revolution against Britain. Whereas her slave poetry reflected a diplomatic position of some neutrality, she later wrote to General George Washington to wish him "all possible success in the great cause" for which he and the other revolutionaries were fighting.[44] She apparently followed closely the events of the war and used them as her themes. Speaking of the Continental Army, Wheatley declares, "Shall I to Washington their praises recite? / Enough thou know'st them in the fields of fight." While Hammon wished for a swift end to the war and emphasized the issue of loyalty between masters and servants, Wheatley expressed her support for the effort with nationalistic pride and a belief in the war's just nature:

> Proceed, great chief, with virtue on thy side,
> Thy ev'ry action let the goddess guide.

A crown, a mansion, and a throne to shine,
With gold unfading, WASHINGTON! Be thine.[45]

Later, in 1784, when Wheatley wrote "An Elegy Sacred to the Memory of That Great Divine, the Reverend and Learned Dr. Samuel Cooper," she describes his dedication not only to God and his congregation but to his country as well: "THY COUNTRY mourn's th' afflicting Hand divine / That now forbids thy radiant lamp to shine." She continues, "Thus COOPER! Thus thy death-less name shall bloom / Unfading in thy *Church and Country's* love."[46] A Boston evangelical active in the revolution, Cooper preached a religion of "spiritual efficacy" and pragmatism and sought to make "worship emotionally satisfying."[47] Although the white Wheatley family certainly had much to do with Phillis Wheatley's activities prior to her manumission, she clearly had a very good understanding of the events of her time and of her role in influencing questions of slavery, liberty, and the future of her country.

Wheatley lived in a time of social turmoil and shifting allegiances. Whereas Hammon found solace in a religion separated from politics, a religion that reviled human efforts as inherently selfish and sinful, Wheatley's writings embraced and developed a set of religious principles that advanced human activity as necessary and even noble if it occurred in the service of equality and freedom. Although Wheatley had previously had numerous communications and connections with hard-line, predestinarian Calvinists who rigidly opposed works as a means to salvation, by 1784 her allegiances seemed to be shifting, allowing "An Elegy on Leaving—" to be published in John Wesley's *Arminian Magazine.*[48] Thus, Wheatley appears to have participated in a theological shift that her past masters and patrons would have found somewhat shocking. Wheatley's name and work were widely known throughout the transatlantic world because of her skill and her dedication to spreading her message of universal freedom and human dignity. Her work also shows, as do the works of John Marrant, Prince Hall, Richard Allen, and Maria Stewart, that black religious writers and evangelicals were actively rethinking, adjusting, and developing their own ideas about religion and society as well as affecting the world around them with those ideas.

CHAPTER THREE

John Marrant and the Narrative Construction of an Early Black Methodist Evangelical

On a cold winter morning, January 27, 1788, John Marrant departed from Halifax, Nova Scotia, for the final time, boarding a ship headed for Boston. For almost three years, he had preached to a dedicated and growing congregation of loyalist blacks who had immigrated there to escape British-American slavery. His goal, as assigned by the Huntingdon Connection of Calvinist Methodists, was to bring a more rigorous predestination doctrine to a region to which the more moderate Wesleyan Methodists, who also vied for control in the area, had previously ministered. He also brought a new covenant, proclaiming himself, through his works and sermons, a prophet and supporting efforts to migrate with his congregation to Sierra Leone to set up a liberated and independent black society, a new Zion. But he did not live to see his congregation depart for Sierra Leone in 1791. Aged beyond his years by wounds suffered during his service in the Royal Navy, the hard life of an itinerant minister, and smallpox, Marrant was buried in a grave adjacent to his church in the London suburb of Islington on April 15, 1791, dead at the age of thirty-five. His autobiographical writings document a life seemingly twice that length in experience, a life throughout which Marrant vigorously sought to build a new society worthy of salvation in the Nova Scotia wilderness and among the black loyalists who fled there after the Revolutionary War.[1] "Marrant did not see Zion built up in his lifetime," observed one commentator. "No prophet, save Enoch, ever has. But he succeeded in constructing a people, a Zion discourse, and a common sense of expectation."[2] On at least two major occasions, Marrant reconstructed himself in sermon and print, first at his ordination ceremony, when William Aldridge and Samuel Whitchurch chronicled and published his sermon, and again upon the 1790 publication of his *Journal*, which describes his exploits in Nova Scotia.[3]

Marrant engaged in the spread of a Christianity tailored to the specific social and political needs of Africans and African Americans living throughout the Atlantic world. Calvinism lay at the foundation of his theology, but the tradition as it was being articulated and practiced at the time was not adequate to the circumstances he wanted to address in his ministry. Therefore, the doctrines he developed and espoused interpreted Calvinism in ways that addressed the specific social and spiritual needs of English-speaking blacks. Principles of equality and social justice grew out of the revolutionary discourse of his time and provided bases for the thinking and practice of black revolutionaries and black loyalists alike.[4] Marrant's emphasis on social and political equality and justice combined with a reworked tradition of the covenanted community, therefore, exemplifies the roots of black theology in America, a theology both of tradition and progressive social change that he offered as "an expansive, inclusive version of a spiritual imperium cleansed of racial hierarchies."[5]

Like many of his Calvinist predecessors, Marrant elaborated on and developed American Calvinism to better address the issues of the time. However, he subscribed to orthodoxy on a number of issues that put him in line with many of his English and British-American contemporaries. One of the major challenges to orthodox Calvinism during the first Great Awakening of 1734–40 was Arminianism—the general belief that humans have the capacity to initiate salvation through their own will. Jonathan Edwards believed his revival work to be a corrective to this type of doctrinal error.[6] George Whitefield's revival also in part constituted a defense of predestination and orthodox Calvinism that upheld the complete sovereignty of God in the process of salvation. Marrant continued the tradition of these well-known evangelicals.

Marrant, like Edwards and Whitefield, emphasized the Pauline tenet of irresistible grace and the subordination of the human will to divine sovereignty. Marrant's emphasis on this doctrine allowed him entrance into one of the major theological discussions of the time and gained him the patronage he needed to be a major missionary voice between England, Nova Scotia, and Boston. However, Marrant also advanced some new theological ideas dangerous to established authority. Marrant's ideas were egalitarian in nature, promoting the dismissal of scholastic pietism in favor of the individual's reading of Scripture. Marrant preached that the New Testament was the sole authority and arbiter between the individual and salvation and that Christians should incorporate their experiences into readings of the Bible. He also advanced extemporaneous or "inspired" preaching and prayer as indicators of one's development as a Christian and of a true connection with God.

Marrant practiced and promoted orthodox principles of Calvinism as one means of attaining a commission to evangelize to a geographically wide-ranging audience. In that effort, Marrant produced two documents that secured his entrance into international revivalism: an ordination sermon that was transcribed into *A Narrative of the Lord's Wonderful Dealings with John Marrant,* and *A Journal of the Rev. John Marrant.* He secured his place in the Huntingdon Connection as an orthodox Calvinist minister through the delivery of the first document. In the second, he advanced his determined faith in predestination while promoting unorthodox doctrines that better suited the spread of Christianity to black congregations and the building of covenanted communities of African peoples that could resist white domination.

Marrant's ordination sermon and journal chronicle physical and spiritual strife. While the countess's organizational imperatives may have offered Marrant an opportunity to enter the Methodist ministry, certain doctrines particular to Huntingdon Methodists probably appealed to his personal sense of identity and helped him explain the often terrible and perilous circumstances of his life. Pious and sincere in his beliefs, he nevertheless knew that he needed to prove his skill and loyalty to the orthodox doctrines of Calvinism to his potential benefactor, Selina Hastings, the Countess of Huntingdon. While Marrant and the countess had different views on the temporal significance of Christianity for free blacks and slaves, he nevertheless addressed his concern for black populations suffering social and spiritual injustice. He did so even when the touchy subject of slavery threatened his relationship with the countess.

In his *Narrative,* for example, he speaks for the first time of his ministry to the slaves on the Jenkins plantation, where Christianity had previously been forbidden to the servants. Using Methodism as his entrée into general discussions of religion and to authorize him as a legitimate evangelical, he addresses and engages in an implicit critique of the American slave system and offers a Christian argument to help ameliorate the conditions of the slaves on the plantation, allowing them more free time to worship and form a community organized around liberatory principles. In his *Journal,* Marrant further preaches a Christianity that incorporates black people and their concerns into the fabric of Christian tradition and history and furthers the legitimacy of worship practices connected to African tradition and community building. His *Journal* includes a 1789 sermon to the African Lodge of Masons in Boston, which adopted Methodism and made Marrant the group's official chaplain. Marrant's efforts further developed black Methodism and Christianity on an international scale and contributed to the building of communities and institutions where black people could assemble to work out principled strategies of resistance.

The goal of founding a model Christian society such as the one that Marrant envisioned was not new to traditional Calvinist covenant theology.[7] Many Puritans as well as other Calvinist sects attempted to establish colonies in the Americas, viewing these new territories as Edens where their own versions of Zion could be established. The British-American religious groups that settled the North American territories included the Puritans, Pilgrims, Baptists, and

Presbyterians. As late as 1753, groups of German-speaking immigrants known as Moravians were still emigrating to the hills of North Carolina to build Christian communities isolated from a sinful secular world. Members of each of these sects believed that their duty included constructing religious societies unblemished by secular authority. This tradition of founding such holy societies on the American continent was almost two centuries old by 1785, and Marrant was a part of that tradition, first in unifying his congregations in the Nova Scotia wilderness and then in encouraging emigration to Sierra Leone.

After his discharge from the British Royal Navy in 1782 at age twenty-six, Marrant spent three years practicing his faith at the Spa Fields Chapel in London, a Dissenting chapel under the protection of the Countess of Huntingdon. Here he began refining his knowledge of Scripture and the duties of an evangelical. Still weakened from the wounds he received while manning a cannon in an engagement with the Dutch off the northeast coast of England, Marrant took a job working for John Marsden, a London cotton merchant. Marrant lived with Marsden during this period and never faltered in his observance of his religious duties. He worked hard for his employer and in his spare time tended to the poor. Marrant "feared God," his employer remarked, "and had a desire to save his soul before he came to live with us;—he shewed himself to be such while he lived with us, by attending the means of Grace diligently, and by being tender hearted to the poor, by giving them money and victuals if he had left himself none."[8] Marrant attended to his worldly duties as a Christian with the vigor of a saint, but he also saw the opportunity to save his soul within the tumultuous and controversial congregation of Spa Fields Chapel.

Long the center of turmoil, Spa Fields Chapel began as an amusement house called the Pantheon, where gentlemen and prostitutes would assemble on Sundays for drink and other activities. By 1776, the proprietor had gone bankrupt, and the building was appropriated and converted into a Dissenting chapel in 1777. The countess acquired the building through legal maneuverings, hoping to make it into an Anglican congregation under her protection. She spent years trying to persuade the Church of England to recognize the chapel, but legitimate, non-Dissenting ministers would have nothing to do with her church, disdaining both her brand of Calvinist Methodism and the aspiring students who attended her Trevecca College. No established religious authorities would ordain her students, feeling that they were underprepared for the ministry and disdaining Methodist enthusiasm. The countess appealed to the Archbishop of Canterbury for the ordination of her students, but he replied in the negative, remarking that Trevecca could not "send forth very able or judicious Divines."[9]

Forced either to abandon her efforts to spread Methodism and reform the Anglican Church from within or to register Spa Fields as a Dissenting church, the countess chose the latter, doing so on January 12, 1782. On March 9, 1783, she authorized her only two ministers to ordain six Trevecca students, thus marking the first moment of separation between her Methodist connection and the Anglican Church.[10] Non-Dissenting ministers of her chapels in Bath and abroad abandoned her en masse, fearing guilt by association. The separation of the Methodist movement from the Church of England and the resulting turmoil also coincided with Marrant's 1782 arrival in London.

Fresh from his military campaigns with the British Navy, Marrant was no stranger to strife and adversity. Nevertheless, it is not yet clear why he chose a congregation and a movement so torn both internally and externally. Perhaps he felt a sense of duty to the connection that had supported Whitefield, the minister who had guided him to salvation one evening in South Carolina when he was fourteen. Or perhaps the chapel's location on the outskirts of London, where he likely lived with his employer, was convenient. Most likely, though, Marrant's decision to join the Spa Fields Chapel resulted from a combination of location, loyalty, and the realization that the church was in dire straits and in need of ministers who could and would preach a doctrine consistent with the countess's beliefs. "I used to exercise my gifts on a Monday evening in prayer and exhortation," wrote Marrant of his activities at Spa Fields, "and was approved of" by the clergy there.[11] In his spare time, Marrant participated in the Methodist ministry at Spa Fields, where his dedication and talents were no doubt recognized as invaluable to the movement, which sorely needed manpower and missionaries who could spread Huntingdonian influence abroad.

Marrant stepped off a British naval vessel, wounded and ailing, after years of hard living aboard warships fighting colonial dissidents and other enemies of the British Crown. He was now a stranger in a foreign land, spiritually as well as physically ailing after abandoning his ministry, which had begun with the native peoples and slaves of the American continent. "I continued in his majesty's service six years and eleven months," he wrote, "and with shame confess, that a lamentable stupor crept over all my spiritual vivacity, life and vigor; I got cold and dead."[12] As Olaudah Equiano later wrote in his autobiography, the harsh life aboard sailing vessels was not conducive to a spiritual life.[13] Whitchurch rendered Marrant's fall in verse:

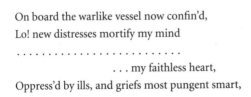

On board the warlike vessel now confin'd,
Lo! new distresses mortify my mind
. . . .
　　　　　　　 . . . my faithless heart,
Oppress'd by ills, and griefs most pungent smart,

Forgot its Lord, and doubt, and fell despair,
And unbelief found entrance there![14]

Whitchurch's poem cites Marrant's fall from grace as part of his testimony. On the British mainland, Marrant renewed his "desire to save his soul" and embarked on a process of repentance that included service to Londoners even poorer and hungrier than himself.

Marrant's account of his evolving life of sin, regeneration, strife, spiritual neglect, repentance, and renewal constitutes a significant aspect of the *Narrative* that conformed to the Methodist interpretation of the Christian life in progress. Although the Methodist doctrine of immediate conversion went against traditional Calvinist Puritan ideals of the Christian life in progress, the Countess of Huntingdon contended that after immediate conversion, a Christian life would be marked by various cycles of crisis that would test the converted. The countess "expected—she demanded—that the true Christian would by definition have to experience a crisis of faith that would perforce prove a never-ceasing series of crises."[15] Because the countess did not want her movement and connection to stray too far from authorized Anglicanism, the "cycle of crisis" doctrine allowed for immediate conversion without neglecting the Christian duty always to strive for and maintain salvation through outward life. Someone with a tumultuous life such as Marrant's could find reason and direction based on this vision of crisis, strife, and perseverance as central evidence of one's selection.

In fact, the direction of Marrant's life probably became clearer as his involvement with the Spa Fields clergy and congregation increased. "During this time," he wrote, "I saw my call to the ministry fuller and clearer; had a feeling of concern for the salvation of my countrymen [in America] . . . for my kinsmen according to the flesh."[16] Although scholars may have neglected and dismissed Marrant because he did not write more about slavery in his *Narrative*, he clearly felt a special bond with the African peoples on the American continent, and he positioned himself to minister to their spiritual and physical needs.[17] Taking advantage of the countess's need for ministers and her passion for overseas missions, Marrant reportedly sent a letter to his brother in Nova Scotia, who replied that "he prayed that some ministers would come and preach to them."[18] Although Marrant had not gone through the religious training usually expected of Anglican or Puritan ministers—he had not learned Latin, ecclesiastical histories, and rhetoric—he nevertheless was at least as qualified for ordination as the other seven students of the countess's Trevecca College ordained that day. Trevecca students often only received a few months' training before being thrust into the ministry. Marrant's clear experience ministering to Indians in their own language and his successful Christianizing of slaves gave him an obvious advantage over his English brethren, who were most likely younger than he and far beneath him in evangelical experience.

As Peter H. Wood has pointed out, Marrant's goals as a Methodist mirrored those of many New Light Puritans the Great Awakening: bringing a "Protestantism which stressed emotional preaching over learned discourse, spontaneous response over rote learning," to the North American frontier, where thousands of black loyalists could gain access to a spirituality that would give definite meaning and direction to what they had previously known as depressed lives of suffering.[19] Many of these people would be liberated slaves looking for help in building a new, free society to which they had previously been denied access. Marrant's loyalist brethren would be in need of common principles by which to organize under hostile circumstances. Marrant saw this opportunity as a chance to bring hope to those who had lost it amid the broken promises of both the American Revolution and the British government.

As Marrant set sail from Nova Scotia for Boston, he likely reflected on the difficulties of building and supporting his mission and the adversity it would encounter. His *Narrative* had gone through ten printings in 1785, the year in which it was first published.[20] By the time he began preaching to the loyalist blacks in Nova Scotia, therefore, a large reading public was already acquainted with the account of Marrant as a precocious youth and itinerant minister of the Gospel. Nevertheless, one of the first difficulties he and his ministry faced was a lack of support and funding from his Huntingdon benefactors despite their pledges to back his efforts. Without the financial and political support of Lady Huntingdon and the connection, Marrant could not hope to build a strong and independent congregation among people who had already been betrayed by the British government, which had denied black immigrants their full share of land grants for their aid during the war with the colonies. Marrant's *Journal* reveals great frustration at the Huntingdon Connection's failure to recognize the importance of the new congregations to which he vigorously ministered. Early in 1788, Marrant may have begun to believe that a place for and support for his ministry existed in the land of his former military adversary, the newly forming American republic, with at least one successful, independent black institution, the African Lodge of Freemasons, that could benefit from his ministerial efforts.

Prior to his ordination, Marrant had had to prove his knowledge and commitment to the doctrines of the Huntingdon Methodists. His faithfulness gained him appointment to go to the land where his brother and other loyalist blacks lived to bring them Christianity in accordance with the set of principles endorsed by the Countess of Huntingdon. However, his loyalty to the Huntingdon ideals was not absolute, and he departed from his Methodist brethren in ways that allowed for the idea of a Zion that fit the particular needs of a principally black and African congregation.[21]

The Americans had abandoned the concept of a covenanted community in favor of New Light theology and universal republicanism.[22] But universal republicanism was not fully egalitarian and did not work for a population that did not fit the dominant social group's definitions of what constituted the universal. As with the case of the Dissenters during a slightly earlier era, the dominant culture considered African Americans outsiders and considered their interests particular and parochial, not universal. The outsider designation and the trials that the majority population heaped on colonial African Americans created conditions under which the covenanted community theology would work particularly well. Like the Hebrews of Exodus, the suffering African Americans endured was easily identified as a sign of their particularity, a trial from God to be endured until they could be delivered. Marrant therefore adapted and developed Huntingdon theology in ways appropriate to the Nova Scotia's black population, giving them a biblical reference with which to understand and endure their suffering as well as a means of developing principles of living while building a community that could resist repression and reap the benefits of God's eventual salvation. This community could also bring balance back to the world by founding Zion in opposition to the sufferings and evil they endured—a New Light principle Marrant built into his ministry.[23]

During his ordination sermon, Marrant related his previous experiences with preaching to African slaves. The beginning of Marrant's ministry to blacks is best known from his *Narrative*, which provides a glimpse into his developing theological views and his careful handling of the politically sensitive issue of slavery, an issue of interest to the slave-owning countess. Marrant reflects on his life just prior to his service in the British Navy. Soon after his conversion, he took a job as a carpenter on a Charleston plantation owned by the Jenkins family and began ministering to the slaves, but the owners, particularly the mistress, took offense, believing that Christianity would "ruin" the slaves. Although the slaveholders had the slaves whipped, they continued to worship, despite being "obliged to meet at midnight in different corners of the woods that were about the plantation." Ambivalent about what to do about Marrant's ministry to the slaves, Jenkins told the young teacher that although he wanted to forbid the slaves from learning Christianity, those who had received such instruction seemed to do their work better than had previously been the case.[24]

This remark seems to reveal Marrant's acquiescence to the idea of the domesticating nature of Christianity. However, it actually reveals a tension or incompatibility between the necessarily desocializing conditions of slavery and Christian principles. Marrant's Christian message, however, was a socializing doctrine, and the Jenkins plantation was one of the first places where Marrant could articulate to a black congregation principles and philosophies that would enable them to organize their lives under extraordinarily violent and oppressive conditions. Like the rest of Marrant's *Narrative*, this section, rather than being an explicitly pro- or antislavery statement, forms part of an explicit construction of what constitutes proper knowledge.

Marrant's spiritual autobiography, which is often studied primarily as a captivity narrative, emphasizes the importance of teaching proper Christian knowledge. Overemphasis on the captivity theme undermines the text's function as a Christian document. In fact, this autobiography, which began as an ordination sermon, articulates Marrant's theology and justifies his participation in evangelical ministries. Making such a justification before the Methodist connection of the Countess of Huntingdon was crucial to his acceptance into the order, where he gained the support he needed to continue his transatlantic ministry.

Marrant understood the social implications the Huntingdon Connection's Christian doctrine and realized Christianity's potential to be an organizing force that could oppose tyranny. However, he also realized that he could not cast himself or his ministry as subversive and still receive support from his benefactors in England. The incident he recounts at the Jenkins plantation shows Marrant purposefully negotiating the tensions between evangelical Christianity and slavery, revealing his knowledge and skill in dealing with the spiritual and secular problems of Huntingdonian Methodism. The British government already regarded Methodism as subversive and conducive to riotous behavior, and Marrant knew that the countess wanted to avoid further suspicion brought on by ministers who criticized government policies and practices. He also knew that the countess was a slave owner, a situation that required him to take care in articulating his case for a North American ministry. His writings offer the opportunity to discover his basic theology as well as how his thinking developed during his intense six years of evangelical work on the American continent.

According to Marrant, he developed a "society" that "increased to about thirty persons" soon after his ministry to the Jenkins slaves began. When Jenkins told Marrant that Christian teaching would "ruin" the slaves as servants, Marrant neither denied the charge nor compromised his principles, methods, or message. Instead, he invoked the doctrine previously set forth by Anglican Church officials and evangelicals that it is the duty of Christians to propagate the Gospel wherever there is a soul in need of salvation and that neglecting this responsibility was an affront to God: "I asked him whether he did not think they had Souls to be saved? He answered yes. I asked him whether he thought they were in the way to save their Souls whilst they were ignorant of that God who made and preserved them. He made me no answer to that. I told him that the blood of those poor Negroes which he had spilt that morning [while whipping them] would be required by God at his hands. He then left me."[25] Marrant clearly knows the arguments for and against preaching to slaves and uses that knowledge to continue his ministry.

This argument regarding the necessity of spreading the Gospel to slaves appears much earlier in Anglican documents. Edmund Gibson's *Two Letters of the Lord Bishop of London* (1727), for example, implore Christians to assist the Society for the Propagation of the Gospel in its missionary efforts by giving serious attention to the teaching of Scripture to slaves. The lord bishop clearly states his disagreement with the majority of colonial planters: "I am loath to think so hardly of any *Christian* Master, as to suppose that he can *deliberately hinder* his Negroes from being instructed in the Christian faith." Moreover, he continues, "The supporting and enlarging of that Church, is justly to be esteemed the *Common Cause* of Christianity, or, in other Words, the general Concern of Christians all the World over."[26] In contrast to the belief that Christianity will make slaves ungovernable, he argues, "In Truth, one great Reason why Severity is at all necessary to maintain Government, is the *Want* of Religion in those who are to be governed."[27] Rather than explicitly defending teaching slaves Christianity on the grounds that doing so domesticates them, Marrant appeals to the Christian's duty to prepare souls for salvation: "By these Means, you will open their Hearts to Instruction, and *prepare* them to receive the Truths of the Gospel; to which if you add a pious *Endeavour* and *Concern* to see them duly instructed, you may become the Instrument of saving many Souls."[28]

Marrant therefore links the pressing question asked by slave owners—Why Christianize slaves?—to their personal salvation, a well-developed Anglican doctrine that he uses to establish his authority as a missionary and evangelical. The adoption of this rationale in the *Narrative* also allows Marrant to avoid ideals that operate to support slavery. Instead, he presents his efforts as primarily spiritual and without regard for the mundane concerns of plantation government, although the doctrine also intersects with the matter of social responsibility. The explicit argument for the domesticating nature of Christianity comes from the mouth of the plantation master, who "could not help acknowledging, that [Christian slaves] did their tasks sooner than the others who were not instructed, and thereby had time after their tasks were done, to keep their own fields in better order than the others, who used to employ the Sabbath for that purpose."[29] But the master does not ask the further question of why the slaves who work so diligently after instruction do so. Rather, Marrant has the plantation owner express rationales for instruction derived from Pauline doctrines articulated by evangelical writers and clerics such as Cotton Mather (in his 1706 defense of slavery in the Massachusetts Bay colonies, *The Negro*

Christianized) and Thomas Coke (who argued in 1738 for the Christianization of slaves in the West Indies in *A Journal of the Rev. Dr. Coke's Visit to Jamaica*). For Jenkins and other members of the slave-owning class, efficiency and plantation government would be most important.

The section of the *Narrative* that chronicles Marrant's ministry to the slaves in South Carolina comes after his story of conversion and Indian captivity and is structured to address the issue of slavery's relationship to Christianity. The *Narrative*'s apparently ambiguous messages regarding his evangelical work make it difficult to determine whether this section operates in an antislavery capacity. On the one hand, Marrant shows the brutality of slavery and the ignorance, particularly of God, that human bondage fosters. On the other hand, the master acknowledges that slaves studied under Marrant are better workers. Ultimately, the plantation owner's wife is punished with sickness and death for trying to deny slaves time for Christian practice, while the ambivalent Jenkins converts and eventually improves the condition of his slaves, allowing them to worship freely, although he never emancipates them.[30]

Slavery would have been a topic of special interest to the countess, who would have watched closely Marrant's handling of this matter, as she did the handling of doctrinal and organizational matters by all of the ministers and churches within her sphere of influence. Marrant would have received special scrutiny because of the countess's previous miscalculations concerning a black minister she sent to her Bethesda, Georgia, plantation to minister to her slaves eleven years earlier.

The countess had never given high priority to Christianizing her slaves or any other slaves. In 1774, however, she attempted to lessen criticism of her involvement with slavery by sending an African minister, David Margate, to minister to the slaves on her Bethesda plantation. She sought to give the appearance of maintaining her duty to spread the Gospel and save the souls of her slaves at a time when people increasingly were questioning the justice of the institution. The decision was also theologically grounded in the proposition that slavery was compatible with predestinarian doctrine. Unlike the Wesleyan Methodists, who contended that slaves lacked access to salvation because they could not exercise free will, the countess's strict predestination doctrine conveniently bypassed will as a condition of salvation as long as the slaves had the proper instruction and baptism. Sending a minister to Christianize her slaves was a defiant message to the Arminian Wesleyans, who repudiated slavery and undermined, in the countess's estimation, the already beleaguered Methodist movement within the Anglican Church. Margate was to be the messenger who delivered the countess's messages and thereby saved and tutored her slaves.[31]

Unfortunately for the countess, Margate ultimately served as a great source of distress to her and the immediate communities of the Bethesda region when he declared himself a new Moses who would lead his people out of bondage. He also began to encourage rebellion and insurrection among the slaves, eventually causing some South Carolina whites to form a lynch party to deal with him. He quickly escaped aboard a ship bound for England, however.[32] The countess undoubtedly wanted to avoid any more such embarrassing and potentially costly mistakes. Marrant's dedication and theology, therefore, had to be sound and had to fall within the bounds of the countess's ideological priorities. The ordination sermon that became the *Narrative* was Marrant's proof that he could be counted on not to cause the kind of trouble that Margate had.

Although this ordination sermon is circumscribed by the editing priorities of the amanuensis, the *Narrative* participates in a long tradition of conversations and sermons arguing for the ameliorating effect of Christianity on the condition of slaves. Marrant's *Narrative* may lack the significance to a contemporary audience that it had for eighteenth-century readers, who would have recognized and contemplated its argument. While Marrant offers little in the way of personal evaluations of the slaves' conditions aside from spiritual matters, the section nonetheless implicitly critiques the slave system by highlighting the legal privileges accorded to free black persons. Marrant's status as a free man shielded him from abuse by Jenkins, who believed he would encounter legal trouble if he acceded to his wife's wishes that he physically abuse his hired carpenter.

Marrant's *Narrative* never indicates that he sought to undermine the plantation's operation, and neither the *Narrative* nor the *Journal* contains any explicit antislavery statements. Scholars have even speculated that Marrant owned a female slave and her two children prior to the 1780 siege of Charleston.[33] But more important for Marrant, adopting an explicit stand against slavery would have alienated him at the beginning from the Methodist connection from which he so badly needed authorization and support. Establishing a belief system that allowed for the propriety of temporal bondage among fellow Christians would have been consistent with the doctrinal and political leanings of the Huntingdon Connection. The Countess of Huntingdon thought slavery a necessary component of society and owned numerous slaves to work her Bethesda mission.[34] Marrant's original spiritual mentor and evangelical colleague, George Whitefield, owned slaves to work his Georgia orphanage and willed about fifty slaves to the countess.[35] Unlike the Wesley brothers, who rejected slavery outright as anti-Christian, Whitefield deferred to the pressure he received from members of his colonial congregations as well as the countess's priorities on the matter. Slavery was acceptable as long as it was nonbrutal and paternalistic. By the time he wrote his *Narrative*, Marrant knew the countess's views on the matter and would not have written in direct opposition to what the connection perceived to be a necessity in Huntingdonian missionary efforts on the American continent.

When Marrant states in his *Narrative* that he goes with his brother to "repair a plantation belonging to Mr. Jenkins," he is saying that he is going to repair the spiritual well-being of the entire plantation rather than the physical buildings.[36] Marrant's apparently paternalistic ministerial relationship with the slaves seems to have had a powerful effect on them. The presence of a free black minister leads the slaves to engage in clandestine activity, worshiping in secret when Jenkins denies them the freedom to follow Marrant's teachings. As several historians have pointed out, such illicit gatherings were common among slaves in the South and the Caribbean who had to hide away in "hush-harbors" to practice religions that their owners believed would "ruin" them.[37]

For the rhetorical purposes of Marrant's narrative record, such disobedient behavior could be tolerated for a while but would ultimately be unacceptable to British citizens profiting from colonial slavery and American audiences who feared that black plots and insurrection would be the outcome of such clandestine meetings. Tensions of this sort in the operation of this text are solved by the death of the wife (a punishment for her anti-Christian denial of the Gospel to the slaves) and Jenkins's conversion, which authorizes the slaves to practice their religion under his supervision. This conclusion to the *Narrative* would have been in keeping with Huntingdonian policy toward slavery and would have made for a more palatable and marketable narrative to American readers and those British who still had a significant stake in Caribbean slavery. The Countess of Huntingdon supported amelioration or the gradual elimination of slavery but did not advocate immediate emancipation. The Huntingdon Connection seems to have vigorously addressed the spiritual needs of slaves and black congregations, directing more efforts toward this end than did the Wesleyans. The countess's ministry certainly included a wide-ranging circle of black Atlantic writers and evangelicals, including not only Marrant and Margate but Equiano and Phillis Wheatley.

Marrant's account of his ministry to slaves in the *Narrative* marks the beginning of what would become his efforts as a prophet and as a leader of his countrymen to Zion. He distances his narrative voice from the concerns of slave owners by focusing on accepted Anglican/Methodist doctrines that highlight the spiritual elements of Christian teaching. Marrant avoids the institutional doctrines that intersect with slaveholders' secular and material concerns, doctrines that explicitly justify or apologize for slavery. However, he complicates matters by revealing that slaves are willing to be disobedient to obtain Christian teaching by stealing to the "different corners of the woods," much in the same way as the early Christians persecuted by the Roman state. To this degree, Marrant disrupts the notions of the domesticating effects of Christianity by highlighting the slaves' covert activities to gain knowledge. This revelation includes an implied threat: If owners do not monitor slaves' religious education, they will seek it themselves, an emancipatory move that threatens the slave system. Unless masters teach the proper forms of the religion, slaves' unmonitored activities could lead to insurrection or further heathenism outside of the dominant culture's control. Of course, who better to do such missionary works than people such as Marrant with "proper" knowledge of the Gospels?

As the *Journal* illustrates, Marrant strongly emphasized proper knowledge throughout his ministry, as did his Methodist connections and benefactors. The statement that Marrant went "to repair a plantation belonging to Mr. Jenkins" has important spiritual implications, since what he recognized as most in need of repair were the souls who inhabited the plantation. Particularly important in the matter of proper Methodist instruction and practice is Marrant's brief but prideful approval of "one of the Negro boys" who had made great progress in the "exercise in extemporary prayer," moving from memorized prayers and catechisms to direct extemporaneous speaking.[38] This short, obscure passage from the text highlights one of the conventions that would later become recognized as a major part of black evangelicalism and that grew out of the syncretism between African oral tradition and Methodist principles of direct inspiration. This ability is another highly valued aspect of black religious speaking and often led to conflicts between educated black ministers and their more vernacular, independent counterparts.[39] Although Marrant frequently argues for proper, Calvinistic interpretations and observance of Scripture, he departs from traditional European norms by privileging oral, extemporaneous sermons over those that are written and carefully delivered.

Marrant saw the limits of a strictly literate, scholastic, formal evangelicalism, particularly among the poorly educated classes and Indians he had already encountered and with whom he remained most involved throughout his career on the American continent. Marrant disdained Christian teaching that hindered a clear knowledge of direct scriptural learning and that limited particular interpretations to an educated elite rather than leaving such interpretations open to each individual. Marrant's beliefs increasingly led him back to the original Calvinist principles of simplicity of service and extended to direct interpretation of the Gospels and expressions of an experiential religion, an approach that put him at odds with other Calvinist sects more concerned with maintaining hierarchy and class distinctions.[40]

His use of a plain, vernacular ministry unrestrained by scholasticism constituted a point of agreement, however, between Marrant and the countess, whose Trevecca students were often encouraged to rush through their studies so that they could preach and engage directly in missionary activities as soon as possible: "Come, come . . . you are only going to a few simple souls: tell them concerning Jesus Christ, and they will be satisfied."[41] Less dogmatic and complicated theologies that "stressed an experiential conversion of the heart rather than an intellectual or catechetical religion" allowed many African peoples in America to identify with a synchronous set of beliefs more congruent with their traditional beliefs and practices.[42] Marrant knew of the origins and spiritual needs of his "countrymen" and developed as a minister who would motivate conversion through a distinct and powerful expressiveness as well as through logic.

Some scholars mistakenly assume that Marrant was illiterate or semiliterate even though he clearly had an aptitude for language and music; his *Journal* also illustrates that he was a meticulous note taker. Although he professed years of formal education, he seems to have retained the vernacular language of his upbringing in South Carolina, a patois that the amanuensis of his *Narrative* thought necessary to alter before putting the document into print: "*I have always preserved Mr. Marrant's ideas, tho' I could not his language; no more alterations, however, have been made than were thought necessary.*"[43] Marrant's vernacular language undoubtedly granted him and his Gospel message greater acceptance among his congregants, who would have seen him less of an outsider because of their shared linguistic patterns. His ministry would have also have been more organic as he negotiated between established doctrine and revealed interpretations of the Bible, unrestrained by scholasticism and dogma and more amenable to other folk patterns and forms of expression.[44]

Although his three years of formal preparation probably made him a better candidate for the ministry than many of the countess's Trevecca students, Marrant's doctrinal disregard for scholasticism led him to disdain publications that he viewed as diluting Christ's message and dividing Christians. Theological treatises by learned men led to disputation and schisms such as those between the Wesleyan and Huntingdonian Methodists as well as the Old and New Light Calvinists. During his evangelical mission in Nova Scotia, Marrant often came into conflict with Wesleyan ministers. On at least one occasion, he had difficulties with a Liverpool, Nova Scotia, New Light congregation that forbade him from preaching to them after hearing one of his sermons that offended the worshipers' sense of doctrine.

Separating himself even more from the mainstream Christian practices of the time, Marrant eventually began to preach against the use of published scholastic doctrine. In the June 1789 Festival of St. John sermon delivered before Boston's Masonic African Lodge, Marrant argues, "Unhappily, too many Christians, so called, take their religion not from the declaration of Christ and his apostles, but from the writings of those they esteem learned.—But, I am to say, it is from the New-Testament only, not from any books whatsoever, however piously wrote, that we ought to seek what is the essence of Christ's religion . . . free from any human mixtures."[45] Marrant has no use for learned, scholastic Christianity, suggesting that individuals—independent of traditional hierarchical authorities—are capable of inspired readings of the Scriptures and that this practice constitutes the center of Christian theology and worship. Most Congregational Christians, particularly the ministers of established churches in a cosmopolitan community such as Boston, would have shunned such ideas because they undermined the ecclesiastical authority earned in school. Marrant launched a direct attack on established doctrines and authority, implying that common folk could glean the meaning of Scripture, independent of established church authorities. By the time Marrant adopted this line of thinking, he was already at odds with his Huntingdon Connection for reasons he did not know and was unable definitively to discover. It is possible that his more independent thinking on issues of authority opened the rift. But while spontaneity and field preaching were established Methodist practice, ideas undermining authority were not in keeping with the countess's ideals and goals. However, these ideas fall into line with Marrant's development as an independent thinker and evangelical whose connections to English patronage had taken a backseat to his commitments to North American African societies and the needs of his black congregations. Even though he went back to England to find answers concerning his lack of support from his former patrons, by 1789 Marrant had established a new set of priorities with a matching theology.

Although it is a part of Marrant's autobiographical account, the section on field preaching to slaves, like the rest of Marrant's *Narrative*, was not designed to represent individualized expression and deep reflection.[46] The *Narrative* presented a theological position by example, offering a firsthand account of an evangelical who sought to expand his ministry to include the American slave population. Like much of the rest of the *Narrative*, this section is didactic in nature. Marrant's personal evaluations beyond the evangelical are secondary to the text's operation as a teaching tool. Marrant seeks to disseminate a lesson that will authorize him as a Methodist minister to bring into existence societies that include or perhaps comprise solely black people living throughout the Atlantic world. But by 1789, his allegiances changed, and his discontent with the Huntingdon Connection found voice in his second published autobiography.

The 1791 *Journal* is the antithesis of the *Narrative*. The earlier work sought to articulate his knowledge and acceptance of Huntingdonian Methodism, whereas the later publication defended his character and evangelical work against charges of dishonesty and corruption leveled by members of the connection. The *Journal* marks the points of schism between Marrant and the Huntingdon Connection, both publicly vindicating his character and announcing his independence as a person and evangelical. Whereas an amanuensis wrote the *Narrative* as a model for conversion and a Christian life, Marrant wrote the *Journal*, intending specifically to address the public at large, which had come to know Marrant and his story five years earlier through his ordination sermon, the *Narrative*, and Whitchurch's *The Negro Convert*.

The opening sentence of the *Journal* begins Marrant's defense: "The following Extracts will shew my readers the impropriety of that report which prevailed so much after I left this country."[47] After three years in Nova Scotia, advancing a strict predestination Calvinist Methodist doctrine, Marrant returned to England in 1788, at great expense to himself, to discover that he had been charged with mishandling Huntingdonian money and that he "was not permitted to speak" for himself and "so remained to the present, without any assistance, or even a Christian word out of them."[48] The preface to his published *Journal* reveals his frustration and feeling that the countess had betrayed him, particularly because he and unofficial, anonymous sources had borne much of the expense of his ministry. Further, he had voluntarily risked life and limb to carry the ministry to the Nova Scotia wilderness, a distinction few others in the connection shared. None of the other seven ministers ordained with him at Bath in 1785 had embarked on such a risky adventure, and Marrant wanted his readers to know the depth of his commitment to spreading the Word of God: "And I am certain of this one thing, that there is not a Preacher belonging to the Connection could have suffered more than I have for the Connection, and the glory of God, and for the good of precious souls."[49]

Even before Marrant departed for Nova Scotia, the financing of his venture had become a point of contention. He received twenty pounds from an unnamed patron to fund his efforts abroad.[50] When he arrived in North America, he found that the people in the community that would serve as his center of operation desperately needed supplies and farming tools: he spent "twenty-four pounds seven shillings" to buy the needed items, with "the greater part of that [money] from the Tabernacle [Chapel] people"—that is, not from the Huntingdonians at Spa Fields.[51] In fact, in his *Journal*, Marrant carefully accounts for his funds to counter the charges that he had squandered the money provided by the Huntingdon Connection.

The Huntingdon Connection distanced itself from Marrant and his mission at its inception. Although William Aldridge published Marrant's ordination sermon as a narrative, helping to popularize Marrant's life and his mission, the connection seemed to lose interest in adequately funding the effort before he left London. The fact that Marrant had a positive relationship with the church leaders at the Tabernacle Chapel would have been seen as a threat to the Countess of Huntingdon's authority over her ministers. She had long been concerned with control and, given her difficulties with Margate, may have reconsidered her patronage of Marrant.

By 1785, the countess had become convinced that the Tabernacle leaders as well as some of Whitefield's other old connections were working hard to steal her ministers and congregation, thus making them "universally to be rejected."[52] Even though Whitefield had been one of the countess's personal chaplains and a highly regarded and valuable member of her connection, his congregations had become objects of suspicion fifteen years after his death. The countess took care to be personally involved and in control of her religious assets. However, she spent most of her time at Spa Fields Chapel. As her relationship with the Tabernacle Chapel declined, she may have perceived Marrant as falling under the influence of her rivals. Accepting donations from the "Tabernacle people" may have instigated the countess's antipathy toward Marrant.

Throughout his career as an evangelist, Marrant was always open to working with Christians whose specific doctrines differed from his own. Although Marrant very much opposed Arminianism and clashed repeatedly with Wesleyan ministers, he did not find their ideas so repugnant that he would not worship alongside them, as he wrote in the *Journal*: "We kept a covenant night on the 1st of January, and so did they; we administered the sacrament again this night, but they did not have anybody to give it to them, for a great many of them came and begged to be partakers with us, and were admitted. Here I staid till the 9th of January, and had a love feast on that night with Mr. Wesley's people, and had a very happy time with them, after which I commended them to God in love."[53] At a time when evangelicals often seemed more interested in arguing than in proselytizing, Marrant was busily building community through his religion rather than disputing fine points of theology. Marrant was less interested in maintaining control of his organization than in spreading principles, and he may have seen the time he spent with the Wesleyans as an opportunity to extend his more orthodox beliefs. Such an approach is certainly in keeping with the evangelical frontier spirit he displays in his *Narrative*.

Marrant's *Narrative* and *Journal* show that his ministry sought to address and encourage social and spiritual equality among black peoples and British Americans. He was not concerned with the factional strife that often preoccupied other ministers, and he certainly attempted to bridge many of the divisions between Methodism and other Christian perspectives by abandoning scholastic methods and Christian teaching, among other efforts to transform Calvinist tradition. Ultimately, however, he sought to develop a Christian ministry and theology that would suit and address the particular social and spiritual circumstances of black people living in postrevolutionary North America. Marrant saw that preaching a Christianity of inclusion and elegance by eliminating unnecessary elaborations on the Scriptures was necessary to bring African-descended people into Methodism. But he also knew that he had to use his sophisticated knowledge of British and British-American Calvinist tradition to convince slave owners and his benefactors that such a ministry was both warranted and practical.

Although his knowledge and use of orthodox and traditional Calvinism enabled him to secure the initial funding for his ministry, he nevertheless taught a progressive Calvinism to his congregants. The language of his ministry is rooted in the discourse of freedom and egalitarianism that black revolutionaries and black loyalists shared. A veteran loyalist who fought in the Revolutionary War and then returned to North America to preach to loyalist immigrants and become chaplain of African Lodge 459 in Boston, Marrant reveals that Christian community, particularly among black people, was far more important than the nationalist or sectarian interests of his day. His writing reveals how he set an example for the development of a black theology that engaged in progressive social action both in principle and in practice. This theology flourished in African American culture and became a part of virtually every major religious institution—and many secular institutions—that developed subsequently.

CHAPTER FOUR

Prince Hall and the Influence of Revolutionary Enlightenment Philosophy on the Institutionalization of Black Religion

Jupiter Hammon, Phillis Wheatley, and John Marrant were black religious writers who worked contemporaneously to change the way black people viewed themselves in relation to religion. Hammon and Wheatley worked primarily as individuals, producing literary expressions of their piety and intellectual engagement with Atlantic culture, whereas Marrant eventually connected himself to larger bodies of black people to express his religious concerns through black institutions—first the interethnic churches of mostly black loyalists living in Nova Scotia, then the African Lodge of Freemasons in Boston. Such coalitions became more common as the free black population grew and coalesced into small communities. African Americans necessarily continued to collaborate with white liberals in struggles for social justice but also assumed more command over the means—both material and rhetorical—by which resistance occurred. The growth of black influence on political activism enabled African Americans to voice concerns that otherwise sympathetic white allies might have overlooked or repressed.

Powerful political and economic institutions emerged in the aftermath of the American Revolution to support the interests of the leaders of the dominant culture; at the same time, African Americans developed institutions to address the social, political, and cultural matters they perceived as important. These institutions dealt with local material concerns such as food and clothing for the poor, labor issues, public education, insurance, and funeral needs as well as the general problems of slavery and political/economic disenfranchisement. The black institutions that developed during the late eighteenth and early nineteenth centuries also provided places of worship as well as fertile sites for social networks, where further black social and political ideas and nascent black nationalism could spread.

The African Masons perhaps constituted the first significant African American institution of this era. Prince Hall adopted the Boston ministry of his former bishop and religious mentor, Marrant, and developed it into part of a tradition of African American liberatory rhetoric that further expanded emerging black Christianity into secular institutions and helped achieve political goals.

As black literacy increased and independent black institutions began to develop, communities of African Americans began to issue calls to end the various forms of antiblack oppression. Such calls and the movements that followed them at the end of the eighteenth century and into the nineteenth legitimized and centered African American identities, ideology, and independence. "Although you are deprived of the means of education," wrote Hall in his 1797 Masonic sermon, "yet you are not deprived of the means of meditation; by which I mean thinking, hearing, and weighing matters, men, and things in your own mind, and making that judgment of them as you think reasonable to satisfy your minds and give answer to those who may ask you a question."[1] Hall's argument for African American rationality and resistance to oppression through the exercise of reason accorded with Enlightenment idealism. The late eighteenth century saw great change in the new nation, and Hall was among those attempting to define the nature of freedom and republican virtue, especially among the black populations, both slave and free, who formed a major part of the national identity.[2]

Writing at the end of the American Revolution, Immanuel Kant defines enlightenment as "man's release from self-incurred tutelage. Tutelage is man's inability to make use of his understanding without direction from another."[3] Hall encourages his readers and listeners to resist this "tutelage" and abdication of intellectual power to established authority. Hall argues that contemplative thought is not the exclusive domain of continental philosophers or British-American political theorists but the heritage of all peoples, African and otherwise, regardless of station. In addition, Hall's "meditation" has a subversive subtext. He warns against "the slavish fear of man, which brings a snare," a distinct appropriation of Kant's statement that tutelage constitutes "not a lack of reason but in lack of resolution and courage to use it without direction from another. *Sapere aude!* 'Have courage to use your reason!'—that is the motto of the enlightenment."[4] Such ideas linking reason, courage, and liberty were widespread in the English world, so much so that Thomas Paine wrote in the *Rights of Man, Part the Second* (1792), "Freedom had been hunted round the globe; reason was considered as rebellion; and the slavery of fear had made men afraid to think."[5]

Like Kant and Paine, Hall links rationality to courage, lending the exercise of independent thought a moral dimension. Throughout his "Charge Delivered to the Brethren of the African Lodge" (1797), Hall appeals to the spirit if not the language of Kant's motto and encourages his audience of black Masons to develop their rational skills. Further connecting rationality, courage, and the pursuit of freedom in material terms, Hall links black rationality and courage to the success of the slave revolt in Saint Domingue (later the Republic of Haiti) by juxtaposing the biblical paraphrase of Ethiopia stretching its hand from slavery to freedom and equality with a statement on the need to "satisfy your own minds" through the exercise and practice of rational thinking. Rationality has much to do with individual ideas and success, but Hall chooses to highlight the public and communal dimension of rationality, its tie to commonly held values such as courage and freedom. Hall underscores this moral aspect of rationality in his "Charge," and after morality is associated with the exercise of the intellect, rationality becomes a communal enterprise, a social practice circumscribed by shared values and the accomplishment of particular goals.

Although Kant never meant his idealism to serve as a basis on which black peoples could authorize and exercise reason, these ideals nevertheless were adapted and articulated for an African American epistemology of understanding and negotiating the world. Whereas Kant, like most philosophers of the era, explicitly privileges the literate over the spoken word as indicative of rational Enlightenment practice, Hall expands the boundaries of rational thought and application to encompass both literate and oral traditions, a move that validates the traditions of African-descended peoples: "This nature hath furnished you with, without letter learning; and some have made great progress therein, some of those I have heard repeat psalms and hymns, and a great part of a sermon, only by hearing it read or preached and why not in other things in nature: how many of this class of our brethren that follow the seas can foretell a storm some days before it comes; whether it will be a heavy or light, a long or a short one; foretell a hurricane, whether it will be destructive or moderate, without any other means than observation and consideration."[6] Hall argues within the sphere of Enlightenment idealism for the legitimacy of various forms of rationality and learning that do not necessarily depend on a literate tradition. This move connects his ideas regarding the nature of rationality to Enlightenment philosophy familiar in British-American culture while simultaneously defining enlightenment in a way that values the orality and folk practices that dominated African and African American culture. Still operating within the boundaries of emerging African American ideologies of identity and agency, Hall inserts elements of Enlightenment philosophy into his ideas of liberal Christianity, thereby constructing a philosophical basis on which blacks may define themselves in an American context on their own terms and in accordance with their own value systems.[7] Hall uses Enlightenment philosophical ideas to justify black independence without relying completely on the assumptions that those ideas already embodied about the nature of rationality. Hall changes the ideas to reflect a value system different from that of European and British Americans. African Americans thus have a philosophical and theological basis on which to speak and write to and for themselves without the aid of an authenticating white authority. Black efforts are authentic on their own terms, as is evidenced by a variety of uses of black rationality that do not necessarily require literacy: "Let those despisers see, altho' many of us cannot read, yet by our own searches and researches into men and things, we have supplied that defect."[8]

Hall, like other black patriots and loyalists of the revolutionary and postrevolutionary periods, embraced republicanism and its ideals of egalitarian social justice. The rhetoric of republicanism, with its promises of freedom and equality, was consistent and inflected with the discourse of Protestant Christianity that was also becoming more widespread among African Americans. Emergent black models of Christianity were abandoning the scholastic and highly stratified notions of Old World Christianity in favor of a conception of religion that highlighted equality among the newly awakened and reborn. This shift resulted partly from Arminianism, with its emphasis on the centrality of humans' involvement in their salvation, but African Americans' understanding of how their particular interests intersected with the values of republican idealism and progressive Christian theologies also played a role. The social forces of revolutionary ideology and theological reform within the Protestant movement worked well with Hall's defense of black ways of knowing as justification for full participation in the political process.

Continental philosophers, revolutionary idealists, and Christian reformers all contributed to an atmosphere of changing relationship between power and the individual in the secular and religious discourse of the time. With African Americans in the thick of these discourses, black literatures illustrate a deep understanding of and participation in all of the arguments of concern to the emerging American nation. At the base of American revolutionary philosophy lay conflicts with Great Britain regarding free trade and parliamentary representation. After those conflicts with Great Britain were resolved and the Continental Congress debated a new constitution, access to cheap and free labor divided the delegation and nearly led to the collapse of the convention. Market forces and a capitalist ethos then dominated U.S. philosophical discourses, and market forces shaped social policy when it came to blacks' role in the new nation.

Among the white Americans negotiating the creation of a new federal government, talk of revolutionary egalitarianism, so popular during the uprising, shifted to the pragmatism of organizing power along economic lines. From these discussions arose new social stratifications that found their way into federal and state legal systems. Legal oppression and the second-class status of Africans and African Americans were codified, establishing a black underclass ripe for social and economic exploitation. This was not an accidental oversight but a systematic reversal of revolutionary ideals that affected many peoples, especially and explicitly blacks, who remained a source of cheap or free labor. However, while white elites consolidated power and political imperatives shifted away from radical republicanism and Enlightenment idealism, African Americans continued to embrace the ideals of revolutionary promise and simultaneously sought to adapt their social and political cultures to address the new organizations of power and anti-Enlightenment resistance.

Hall's invocation of the Haitian Revolution represented neither an idle passing reflection nor a remark that a white amanuensis or most sympathetic white abolitionists would find acceptable. Black sermons and pamphleteering therefore assume the distinct quality of independence from white authority and develop a rhetoric of resistance with a logos constructed around tropes positively valued and generated by secular and religious black experience. For example, Hall's statement, "Thus doth Ethiopia begin to stretch forth her hand, from a sink of slavery to freedom and equality," eloquently encapsulates a secular reference to successful black revolution with biblical exegesis, a reading of the Scriptures that gives a positive religious and historical justification to active resistance to slavery. Hall's reading of this biblical passage contrasts with previous interpretations that code Africa as a passive actor in a drama where African peoples are reaching toward European benevolence and white assistance. Rather, Hall's reading reveals Africa's outstretched hand as its own liberating force, pulling itself and all African peoples out of slavery.

Hall's interpretation of Psalms 68:31 extends the revolutionary impulse that fueled the American resistance as well as the slave rebellions in the West Indies. By design, this interpretation codifies black identity and agency as authorized by the Bible, the infallible Word of God. White Americans, both pro- and antislavery, viewed the Haitian Revolution as a frightening and terrible event, a blow to proslavery arguments of inferiority on the one hand and an inspiration for white fears of black violence in the name of liberty on the other. Slaveholders feared the example the Haitian Revolution set for violent resistance, and abolitionists feared the popular backlash of embracing the revolt as a model of justice. African Americans read the revolution and interpretations such as Hall's as the unfolding of biblical prophecy and a vindication of the ideals of radical republicanism and egalitarianism that were being abandoned by the dominant white culture in favor of a safer and more accommodating gradualism. In 1795, Peter Williams Sr. led a group of black congregants out of New York's

John Street Church to protest "black pews" and the "continued white racism against the Haitian revolution." A year later, this group of black dissidents constructed the African Methodist Episcopal Zion Church.[9] News of the Haitian Revolution reverberated through North America, influencing public policy, affecting foreign policy, leading to the tightening of slave codes, and providing African Americans with a model for resistance. Attitudes about the significance of the Haitian Revolution even divided black citizens from otherwise sympathetic whites, prompting African Americans to build and take greater control of their social and political destiny. Like Marrant's 1789 sermon and 1790 *Journal* and the black congregants' 1795 New York walkout, Hall's 1797 "Charge" refuted and challenged white authority.

Black autobiography was a unique and popular genre that began to develop during the second half of the eighteenth century. It had a valuable impact on the imagination of antebellum Americans and contributed to the antislavery movement by presenting readers with cold, harsh representations of slavery in practice. As William L. Andrews has pointed out, "Afro-American literature of the late eighteenth and early nineteenth centuries is dominated by treatises, pamphlets, addresses, and appeals, all of which employ expostulatory means to confront the problem of the black situation in white America. Yet only black autobiography had a mass impact on the conscience of antebellum Americans."[10] Yet answering the question of why this particular type of black writing dominated as a literary form is difficult. According to Andrews, even contemporaneous sympathetic readers would find the "most reliable slave narrative [to be] one that seemed purely mimetic, in which the self is on the periphery instead of at the center of attention, looking outside not within, transcribing rather than interpreting a set of objective facts."[11]

The majority of these slave narratives that enjoyed the approval of the white antislavery establishment thus focused on the "objective facts" of slavery rather than on individuals' ideas and interpretations. In other words, discussions centered on oppression rather than on those who suffered from it. Marginalizing and even muting black narrators' voices enabled white abolitionists to impose their priorities on the texts and the antislavery movement. The result is a literature that while definitely antislavery was not necessarily proequality. Even some of the most outspoken immediatist abolitionists, such as William Lloyd Garrison, did not necessarily see a contradiction between antislavery and accepting African Americans as second-class citizens. This ideology is reflected in the genre constraints that he and other white abolitionist leaders placed on black writers and orators, requiring them to tell their stories without elaborating about what their experiences may have meant to them personally.[12] The most well-known example of white abolitionist disregard for an explicit black sensibility in narratives occurred between Garrison and Frederick Douglass. In *My Bondage and My Freedom*, Douglass explains the difficulties he encountered when he attempted to develop his life story beyond a simple recitation of facts:

> "Give us the facts," said Collins, "we will take care of the philosophy." . . . "Tell your story, Frederick," would whisper my then revered friend, William Lloyd Garrison, as I stepped upon the platform. I could not always obey, for I was now reading and thinking. . . . It did not entirely satisfy me to *narrate* wrongs; I felt like *denouncing* them. I could not always curb my moral indignation for the perpetrators of slaveholding villainy, long enough for a circumstantial statement of the facts which almost everybody must know. . . . These excellent friends were actuated by the best of motives, and were not altogether wrong in their advice; and still I must speak just the word that seemed to *me* the word to be spoken *by* me.[13]

The result of Douglass's insistence on defining his philosophy and speaking unmediated words was a split between him and Garrison that led Douglass to develop a separate branch of the antislavery movement and the 1855 publication of his much more developed and contemplative work.

The slave narrative gained its relative popularity over unmediated sermons, pamphlets, petitions, and appeals as a consequence of this struggle for control of the terms by which black experiences would be represented when black writers and activists sought to present their cases. Many white abolitionists objected to the fact that black activists often wanted not only to speak out against slavery in their writing but also to encourage and practice ideas of equality. Such a philosophy required that black people play a greater leadership role within the movement and any institutions resulting from successful abolitionist activism. It also meant that the general abolitionist movement would have to acknowledge that the revolutionary ethos that led to the militant American resistance was as valid a response to slaveholding tyranny as to the excesses of British imperialist policy.

Most white abolitionists were frightened by the implications of African American freedom and equality; although sympathetic to blacks' plight, even these whites were not yet ready to abdicate power or to examine critically their complicity in oppressive American social practices. A deeper study of the contradictions of the American social and political systems and a significant challenge to them ultimately came from more independent voices backed by institutions of emerging black Christianity and secular authority. While these voices did not receive the widespread popular attention accorded to most slave narratives, they nevertheless had profound influence. Sermons and pamphlets such as Hall's also provide an opportunity to further plumb the depths of African American intellectualism. While the white-led abolitionist movement did its part to bring about an end to slavery, organizations such as the African Masons did double duty, encouraging an end to slavery and the spread of social, cultural, and political equality.

Prince Hall wrote two public speeches, called charges, one in 1792 and the other in 1797. The lessons of equality Hall expressed in the two charges can be traced back to the example of Marrant's sermon delivered to the African Lodge during the 1789 Festival of St. John the Baptist. Marrant uses the Bible, particularly the New Testament, as his basis for authority to comment on social practices of the period, just as Hall did several years later. Further, Marrant appropriates themes and the teachings of revered saints to construct a double-voiced sermon that disrupts assumptions about white supremacy and positions Africans and African Americans as the equal of all other true Christians. This sermon traces a history of African involvement in Masonic tradition and argues for the equal rights of blacks on the basis of that history. Marrant opens with passages from the book of Romans, written by the apostle Paul, who also wrote the passage in Ephesians 6:5–6 advising servants to be obedient to their masters. As chapter 1 discusses, advocates of slavery often used that passage to argue that slavery was consistent with Christianity. Marrant, however, uses Romans, Paul's most systematic account of his understanding of the Gospels, to argue for the significance of Christianity in individual lives and in society as a whole: "The apostle here sets down . . . to love one another sincerely, to be ready to all good offices—to sympathize in the good or evil that befalls our brethren, to comfort and assist those that are in affliction and to live together in a spirit of humility, peace, and unity."[14] Such teachings, a lesson on how a Christian society should operate, problematize the notion of slavery and its legitimacy of slavery.

As Richard Newman, Patrick Rael, and Philip Lapsansky have stated in *Pamphlets of Protest* (2001), "Emerging during a period of rapid change in the new American nation—a nation black colonists helped create but were not fully part of—the first generation of black pamphlet writers claimed a space in the Republic by fighting for their rights in print."[15] Three years after the ratification of the U.S. Constitution, African Americans, many of them veterans of the Revolutionary War, lacked the right to participate in civil government. Although those blacks who owned property were required to pay taxes and were counted toward a state's congressional representation, free African Americans still could not vote, and legislative bodies ignored their concerns. Hall's writings indicate a worsening of black-white relations in many respects in Boston and the surrounding region, describing white-on-black violence as well as a rise of colonizationist ideas among whites that caused him to reconsider his position on the subject.[16]

The slave trade, as it operated on the American continent, expanded immensely between 1680 and 1800. As John Thornton has explained in his groundbreaking study of African relations with Atlantic European nations, *Africa and Africans in the Making of the Atlantic World, 1400–1800* (1998), "From about 36,000 persons a year at the beginning of the century, the trade had more than doubled by the 1760s, and it reached a high point of nearly 80,000 per year in the last two decades of the century."[17] Slavery remained a rampant and growing institution even after the ratification of the Constitution: South Carolina, for example, imported more than 40,000 African slaves between 1803 and 1808.[18] Even after it was banned in 1808, the slave trade continued to expand via the clandestine importation of captured Africans and the internal slave trade, fueled by the establishment of world markets for American textiles and the opening of new territories to westward expansion. By 1820, the U.S. slave population had tripled since the beginning of the American Revolution.[19]

In addition to opposing slavery and disenfranchisement, black protesters pushed for greater access to public education, a goal blocked by whites who argued that black people were suited for menial labor jobs and that a liberal education would be superfluous for such a workforce. Hall made education central to his activism, as did many of his followers who also wrote protest pamphlets and essays. Education therefore became a focal point as black populations expanded and African Americans sought broader rights and citizenship in the new republic.

Hall addresses all of these concerns. Speaking at the 1792 Festival of St. John the Baptist, Hall acknowledges his intellectual debt to his predecessor and spiritual guide: "It is requisite that we should on these public days, and when we appear in form, give some reason as a foundation for our so doing, but this has already been done, in a discourse delivered in substance by our late Reverend Brother *John Marrant*, and is now in print."[20] Building on Marrant's foundation, Hall begins to speak concretely about the duties of a Mason, beginning with a belief "in one Supreme Being" and moving on to state that "we must be good subjects to the laws of the land in which we dwell, giving honour to our lawful Governors and Magistrates, giving honour to whom honor is due; and have no hand in any plots or conspiracies or rebellion, or side or assist in them."[21] At first sight, this passage might seem accommodationist, but Hall was responding cautiously to the turbulent politics of the time, when rebellions were resulting from the bleak financial situation of overtaxed citizens burdened with repaying the revolution's war debts. Shays' Rebellion broke out in Massachusetts in late August 1786 when farmers refused to allow the local courts to foreclose on their property to be used as capital with which to pay down the war debt. The rebellion was quelled by February 1787, but not until after it revealed the weakness of a government in need of significant reform. Such events—combined with Spain's closing of the Mississippi in 1784, the presence of illegal British military posts in the Northwest, from which attempts to persuade Vermont to become a Canadian province were made, and the outbreak of the Haitian Revolution in 1791—only increased the difficulties of governing the new republic.[22] Rather than claiming that his audience had a duty to act rebelliously within this chaotic atmosphere, Hall appeals to loyalty and peaceful resolution to the difficulties faced by African Americans at a time when political organization and enfranchisement were still seen as negotiable.

The appeal to civil obedience again echoes Marrant's sermon, which described peace as existing "where Masonry most abounds" and where subjects always conform "to the laws of that country in which they reside, always willing to submit to their magistrates and rulers."[23] In addition to responding to the turbulence of the times, Hall attempts to honor Marrant's contribution to the African Lodge's sense of purpose by practicing the Masonic mandate of community and mutual obligation. But the obedience of which Hall speaks does not come uncritically, for the mandate does not argue that one should turn a blind eye to the contradictions and excesses of an American bigotry that diminished the nation's possibilities.

While Hall's "Charge" was originally directed to the African Lodge, its message was intended for all Masons, regardless of race. Solomon's building of the Temple of Jerusalem remained the model for proper Masonic conduct, and all members of the order should aspire to mutual "love and benevolence to all the whole family of mankind" in building the new nation. Hall reminds his audience of the potential "rebellion" between Lot's and Abraham's servants until Abraham restored peace by dividing the land equally between the two tribes, "for the land is before us," Hall paraphrases, "if you go to the left, then I will go to the right. . . . They divided and peace was restored."[24] Although this passage may be read as a protonationalist statement, within the boundaries of republican egalitarianism it actually represents an appeal for a more equal distribution of wealth. This was not such an unusual idea at a time when war debts, lapsing mortgages, and high taxation were making many citizens miserable. In France, Paine wrote in *Agrarian Justice* (1795) that in its natural state, the earth was "the common property of the human race" and that the tax system should provide payment to every adult "as compensation for the unequal distribution of land."[25] "It is not charity," wrote Paine, "but a right—not bounty but justice, that I am pleading for."[26] According to Paine, unequal distribution of property and the lack of universal male suffrage constituted the main culprits behind human misery, and these two problems were important to African American Bostonians, who suffered disenfranchisement, taxation, and poverty. Most American blacks were even worse off as slaves who did not even own their own bodies. So Hall's allusion to Abraham's solution to "rebellion" was not an argument for separation of the races or nationalism but an appeal to the wisdom of more equitable wealth distribution and equalization of the political process. It is an instance that concerns how to deal with civil strife in a peaceful, egalitarian manner grounded on the principles set forth in the Bible, according to which Christians should regulate their affairs.

However, this passage also raises the specter of rebellion should the American government and the state of Massachusetts decide to ignore the teachings of the Holy Writ. While the introduction to Hall's 1792 "Charge" teaches civil obedience and how "lawful Governors and Magistrates" ought to act, it implies that to act contrary to the Scriptures is to invite discord.

At a time when the United States was still vigorously debating the justice of slavery and southern states were importing slaves to the continent in record numbers, the fear of slave insurrection weighed heavily on the minds of plantation owners, governors, and local and federal authorities. Throughout the seventeenth and eighteenth centuries, slave insurrections and rebellions by runaway-slave communities in the island colonies and Brazil kept Europeans fighting. "Indeed, it is probably safe to say," Thornton has reflected, "that the European colonists spent as much time and military energy fighting runaways and invading their territory as they spent fighting Native Americans along the unconquered frontier."[27] So much military effort was expended to control rebellious slaves because "a large percentage of the slaves were captured in wars and thus had at least some experience with African military systems."[28] While most of the well-known rebellions took place in the Caribbean, Brazil, and the Spanish South, insurrection was not unknown in the North American colonies and, according to Herbert Aptheker, was far more widespread than is commonly believed or studied. As Aptheker has pointed out, "While there is a difference of opinion as to the prevalence of discontent among the slaves, one finds very nearly unanimous agreement concerning the widespread fear of servile rebellion."[29] The generally low number of known rebellions in British North America may be explained by the fact that during the eighteenth century, North America received only 6 percent of the slave imports in the Atlantic world.[30] Nevertheless, the number of slaves coming in by the end of the eighteenth century, coupled with the possibility of the spread of slavery into western territories, which would need to be defended from potential insurrections, affected national policy. The Northwest Ordinance, which provided for the creation of present-day Illinois, Indiana, Michigan, Ohio, Wisconsin, and parts of Minnesota, was passed under the provision that these territories would not become slave states, in large part because the federal government did not want the responsibility and expense of providing militias to defend against slave insurrections, an obligation that was later incorporated into the U.S. Constitution.[31] Militarization was a profound feature of the American South that did not go without international recognition, and white Americans became increasingly concerned with the subject as the black population grew.[32] Southern political officials sought to control potential rebellions by organizing a police state and restricting the movement of black people; northern states, in contrast, used judicial and economic means to subdue and control black populations. The failure to spread social and political liberties would result in dire consequences. Five years after his 1792 "Charge," Hall followed with another one that more explicitly lays out the complaints of Boston's black population.

Although Hall's 1792 "Charge" laid out a complaint against bigotry, it was more an argument for social order and an expression of Masonic duties within a Christian society. His 1797 speech, delivered on the day of the Festival of St. John the Baptist, contained a more comprehensive and pointed argument against the bigotry and oppression of black people—a much more explicit and nuanced argument. Of particular importance are Hall's arguments for the necessity of greater black access to public education. The 1792 "Charge" focused on social obligations and addresses the issue of education only obliquely and in passing. Near the close of the first "Charge," Hall tells his audience, "Let us lay by our recreations, and all superfluities, so that we may have that to educate our rising generation, which was spent in those follies." If blacks work to educate their children, "who knows but God may raise up some friend or body of friends, as he did in *Philadelphia*, to open a school for the blacks here, as that friendly city has done there."[33] Hall refers to the Philadelphia African School, organized by the Quaker abolitionist Anthony Benezet in 1782. Moreover, Philadelphia was a "friendly city" because of the Free African Society of Philadelphia, organized in 1787 by former slaves Absalom Jones and Richard Allen with the ultimate goal of founding an independent black church. The presence of such an auspicious and active body of black activists would have led Hall to perceive Philadelphia as a tolerant place for African Americans. This brief mention constitutes the only real reference to education in Hall's comparatively short first "Charge."

Hall's second "Charge," however, opens with a complaint regarding the difficulties encountered by Boston's African American citizens. Hall states immediately that this particular "Charge" is about "the duty to sympathize with our fellow men under their troubles, the families of our brethren who are gone. . . . But my brethren, although we begin here, we must not end here; for only look around you and you will see and hear numbers of our fellow men crying out to holy Job, Have pity on me."[34] In the rest of this "Charge," Hall calls on his audience to remain calm and resolute in the face of racist violence and indifference: "Let us pray to Almighty God, while we remain in the tabernacle, that he would give us the grace of patience and strength to bear up under all our troubles." Despite the increased physical and psychological violence against blacks in Boston's climate at the time, Hall counseled patience, "for were we not possess'd of a great measure of it you could not bear up under the daily insults you meet with in the streets of Boston; much more on public days of recreation, how you are shamefully abus'd, and that at such a degree that you may truly be said to carry your lives in your hands, and the arrows of death are flying about your heads; helpless old women have their clothes torn off their backs, even to the exposing of their nakedness."[35] These threats and insults, which were not hyperbole, were further compounded by the constant public humiliation of buffoonish caricatures of black people posted throughout the city. Peter P. Hinks has noted that on any given day, shop and tavern windows displayed innumerable cartoons that "ridiculed African American physiognomy and culture in the most humiliating and vulgar manner."[36] Black activist Hosea Easton, a contemporary of Hall, wrote that "cuts and placards of the Negroe's deformity are everywhere displayed. . . . Many of the popular bookstores, in commercial towns and cities, have their show windows lined with them. The bar-rooms of the most popular public houses in the country, sometimes have their ceiling literally covered with them."[37] In addition to such caricatures, the growing free black populations also encountered violence in the form of antiblack race riots throughout the country.[38] Hall quotes a "gentleman" who claimed that "he never saw so cruel behavior in all his life, and that a slave in the West-Indies, on Sunday or holidays enjoys himself and friends without molestation."[39] Although Hall exhorts his audience to be patient during this time of crisis, he does not instruct them to be complacent. He makes clear that it "'tis not for want of courage in you" that the violence is occurring, but to avoid disgracing their community, African Americans should nevertheless obey state laws prohibiting mob assemblies.[40] He reminds them of the courage displayed by the successful slave revolt in Haiti, an example of "Ethiopia [stretching] forth her hand, from a sink of slavery to freedom and equality."[41] Tension arises between the Hall's statements encouraging obedience to civil law and his threats of black violence against white oppressors, which he implies are the just desserts of oppressive regimes. But Hall's primary solution to oppression is the pursuit of knowledge—by becoming educated, African Americans can advance toward the goal of equality and social justice.

In large part, Hall's 1797 "Charge" articulates an African American epistemology as a means by which his listeners can comprehend their role as intellectual beings within British-American culture. He also advances a way of thinking about knowledge that challenges the aesthetic expectations of the dominant culture, which clearly depreciates African American lives and lifeways. Hall believes that this problem can be solved largely by linking knowledge with Christian virtue and Christian virtue with aesthetics—in particular, an African American aesthetic informed by the Christian values he advocates in both his speeches. Hall most succinctly theorizes his black Christian aesthetic in the poem that concludes his 1797 "Charge":

> Let blind admirers handsome faces praise,
> And graceful features to great honor raise,
> The glories of the red and white express,
> I know no beauty but in holiness;
> If God of beauty be the uncreate
> Perfect idea, in this lower state,
> The greatest beauties of an human mould
> Who most resemble Him we justly hold;
> Whom we resemble not in flesh and blood,
> But being pure and holy, just and good:
> May such a beauty fall but to my share,
> For curious shape or face I'll never care.[42]

This poem comments on the nature of beauty, resisting racist caricatures and attacks on African American physiognomy and concepts of what is attractive. Just as he defends and promotes black oral tradition and forms of knowledge as legitimate practices of rationality, he also establishes a system for appreciating African American forms of beauty. The concept of holiness, just like reason, duty, and society, is connected to spiritual values. Hall critiques not only white ideals of beauty but also those of Native Americans. Since much of the dominant culture has identified Native Americans as pagan but nevertheless noble, Hall's poem implies that British-American concepts of beauty have drifted away from a Christian, spiritual foundation to one more in common with perceived Indian idolatry. Hall's British-American readers would have immediately recognized this collapsing of white and Native American aesthetics as an accusation of the influence of vulgar secularism and even paganism on white culture. At the same time, Hall affirms the African American view that "holiness" is the measure of beauty, a view that further connects blacks to the common vision of a Christian aesthetic that should unite them. Eighteenth-century readers would have read the word *uncreate* as *uncreated*. That line of the poem joins with the following one to build off of Hall's use of "holiness" as a standard, arguing that God, uncreated and eternal, is perfection and that the closest human cognates "in this lower state . . . most resemble Him we justly hold." Hall's *we* is understood to be the black people who have withstood white bigotry and oppression with Christian patience and adherence to the rules of society. Although they, or anyone else, for that matter, may not resemble God "in flesh and blood," by "being pure and holy, just and good," they come close to holy perfection.

"May such a beauty fall but to my share, / For curious shape or face I'll never care." Hall emphasizes spiritual considerations in the contemplation of aesthetic beauty but does not completely abandon the physical realm, arguing that the "greatest beauties of an human mould . . . we justly hold." This poem validates black beauty without overemphasizing its physical manifestations. Rather, Hall has decided to remain on a theoretical level, making the religious argument for beauty that will further open a space in American print culture in which he can argue for the physical, intellectual, and social equality of African Americans.

Hall made African Lodge 459 a center for black leadership in which future writers and organizers including Richard Allen, David Walker, and Maria Stewart learned and developed their ideas regarding equality and spread their viewpoints. Many of the founders of the important African American institutions examined in this book began their lives as slaves—among them Hall, Allen, and Jones. Hall was one of the first former slaves to build an enduring American institution of great social and political significance. However, other black leaders, both former slaves and those born free, followed Hall's example and sought to form separate social and religious institutions.

CHAPTER FIVE

Richard Allen and the Further Institutionalization of Black Theologies

Richard Allen was the founder of and the first bishop in the African Methodist Episcopal (AME) Church, the first independent black denomination in North America. Scholars generally believe that the African church movement began in 1792 or 1793, when the black members of St. George's Methodist Church in Philadelphia walked out as a group as a consequence of intolerable discrimination within the predominantly white church. Church officials had ordered the black members to sit in a recently added gallery at the back of the church, but when they kneeled to pray, officials directed them to move to the back of the gallery. The black congregants intended to finish praying before moving, but the irate trustees tried forcibly to roust them. After they finished praying, the black members "all went out of the church as a body," never to return to St. George's.[1]

This walkout is generally hailed as the moment when black Philadelphians began the independent religious movement that resulted in the creation of the AME church, but while this scene of clear-cut discrimination and black resistance might be memorable, the story has, as Albert Raboteau has pointed out in *A Fire in the Bones*, "influenced historians to overemphasize white racism as the reason for the development of the black church."[2] In fact, one of the black congregants who walked out, Richard Allen, had proposed the formation of a separate black church as far back as 1786. At the time, however, the black and white colleagues to whom Allen proposed the plan almost universally rejected it. Further, most of the black members of St. George's were there because Allen's ministerial work had drawn them to the church, so his efforts as an evangelist had helped to form the body of black congregants. Rather than springing from discrimination, the idea of an independent black church in Philadelphia originated long before the walkout at St. George's.

Many factors—social influences as well as influences personal to Allen—contributed to the independent black church movement. His background and

place in history made him the catalyst that initiated a large regional social movement that spread to encompass the nation in his lifetime and subsequently
flourished for more than two centuries. As the eminent scholar and theologian
William Ragsdale Cannon has remarked in his study of John Wesley's theology,
"Any movement, by reason of the very fact that it is a movement and exerts
influence, bears the marks of its own age and reflects the temper of the times in
which it was launched. In the crisis of political and social history, the problems
at hand call forth their own solutions."[3] For Allen's independent black church
movement, slavery and oppression figured large, but many other factors, including a general philosophical shift toward the ideals of radical republicanism
and Enlightenment rationality coupled with Allen's understanding of African
American culture, also contributed. While none of Allen's sermons has survived, his extant writings offer much information, explaining the circumstances
that led to his involvement in the development of one of the most influential
institutions for black America.

By 1792, the trustees of St. George's were becoming concerned about the
growing number of black congregants regularly attending the church and were
becoming increasingly hostile to their presence. In February 1786, Allen came
to St. George's from his post in Radnor, Pennsylvania, recruited by an elder of
the Philadelphia circuit of Methodist ministers to preach to the small number
of blacks attending the Philadelphia church.[4] Allen's account of his itinerant
ministry indicates that he was content as a wandering Methodist evangelist,
mentored by and collegial with many of the denomination's most prominent
ministers circulating in British North America. Although in some regions he
found the people "dead to religion," he never complained about the conditions
of his Gospel labors until he arrived to preach at St. George's, where he was
expected to hold service at five o'clock in the morning: "I strove to preach as
well as I could, but it was a great cross to me; but the Lord was with me."[5] Allen's
efforts bore fruit. By the end of the year, the small number of black congregants
had grown into a "society" of forty-two members.[6] Over the next six years, the
members of this group and the other blacks who later joined them became more
involved in the church's development.

As Allen relates in his autobiography, *The Life, Experience, and Gospel Labours
of the Rt. Rev. Richard Allen*, the black congregants worked to improve and en-
large the building, including helping to build the new gallery and laying new
floors.[7] But not long thereafter, the walkout occurred: "Just as the house was
made comfortable, we were turned out from enjoying the comforts of worshipping therein."[8] The fact that church authorities had welcomed black funding
and labor yet denied African Americans equal treatment within the church was
not lost on Allen and his friends, many of whom were former slaves. Allen's

autobiographical account makes it seem as if the walkout was spontaneous, but evidence shows that the black congregation's reaction may have been part of a larger plan to leave St. George's. Although the church trustees and other ecclesiastical authorities discriminated, they did not want to lose the black members altogether, which would result in the loss of valuable tithe revenue. Church officials also did not want to see the creation of a competing black church because, as Allen well knew, a separate house of worship would call into question the authority of white church leaders, especially if black ministers who shared religious authority led those churches. A relationship between separate and independent white and black churches would further imply social equality among Christians regardless of race. While doctrine might dictate that whites and blacks were spiritually equal in the eyes of God, such equality did not extend to the church's temporal social organization.

The St. George's incident occurred at a moment in the nation's history when egalitarian tendencies were being abandoned in favor of the ideals associated with a stronger centralized federal government. Other institutions, including the church, also reflected this tendency. During and immediately after the American Revolution, churches were much more open and accepting of ideals of equality, a consequence of Americans' overriding concern with repression. This concern subsequently diminished, however, and whites came to expect black people passively to receive religion and government rather than to participate actively in those institutions.[9] White ministers—particularly Methodist ministers, whose denomination had consolidated under a single general conference in 1784—went to great lengths to prevent the development of a fully independent black church in Philadelphia, but in August 1794, black Philadelphians dedicated St. Thomas's African Protestant Episcopal Church. Preparations for an African church had begun in earnest at least a year before the walkout occurred, as Allen and other leaders approached one of Pennsylvania's foremost revolutionaries, Benjamin Rush, in 1791, seeking aid in acquiring funds for the construction of the building that would house the black congregation. Questions seem to have arisen early in the planning process about the new congregation's denomination. Rush wrote to his wife of his belief that the church's "principal contributions will come from the Deists," indicating that established denominations and their members were not forthcoming in support of a black church.[10] Even Philadelphia's Quakers had difficulty coming to terms with the presence of a distinct African church, denying Allen's followers even temporary permission to worship in a Quaker schoolhouse because, according to Rush, "part of their worship consisted in singing psalms."[11] Several weeks later, Rush wrote to Granville Sharp, an English scholar and powerful abolition activist who had met and entertained Phillis Wheatley almost two decades earlier, that the representatives of the planning committee had "formed Articles and a Plan of Church Government so general as to embrace all, and yet so orthodox in cardinal points as to offend none."[12] The effort to "offend none" reflects a tension between Allen's desire to form a Methodist society and resistance from the rest of leaders of the black congregation that is a major theme in Allen's autobiography. While plans moved forward to acquire funds and determine church government for the project, the incident at St. George's that precipitated the walkout apparently provided the final material proof needed to justify separation. By the end of May 1794, the African church was almost complete and ready for dedication. But Allen had excused himself from the project of forming this church late that spring as a consequence of the group's decision not to follow Allen's wishes regarding denominational affiliation. Allen contended that "there was no religious sect or denomination [that] would suit the capacity of the coloured people as well as the Methodists."[13] Nevertheless, the members of the church voted to align with the Episcopal Church of America.

Undaunted by the result and adamant in his conviction that Methodism best suited African Americans, Allen immediately began making plans to erect yet another separate church. In May, Allen and his followers purchased a frame structure and moved it to Sixth and Lombard Streets, where it was dedicated by Bishop Francis Asbury of the AME Conference in July.[14] Not yet even an official administrator within an established denomination, Allen had already founded two black churches and the Free African Society, which oversaw the financing and building of the African church and provided relief services. "I was the first proposer of the African church," Allen reminds his readers in his autobiography. "I put the first spade to ground to dig the cellar for the same."[15] He then went on to build what would become Bethel African Church. Not until five years after Bethel's dedication did Asbury ordain Allen a deacon of the church, but he had taken the first significant steps toward becoming the founding bishop of the first independent African American denomination.

What inspired this flurry of activity that led to the founding of black churches and later the AME denomination? Although others, such as Allen's friend, Absalom Jones, and mentors within the Methodist movement, aided Allen, his tenacity and dedication to ecclesiastical independence for African American Christians culminated in one of the most profound social movements in American history. Allen was moved not solely by oppression but also by initiative, and having lived through the tumultuous American Revolution, he likely took the ideals of independence and sovereignty very seriously and extended them to African Americans, who sought literal liberty and independence from the demands and priorities of British-American interests. On December 30, 1799, Jones, then the pastor at Philadelphia's St. Thomas's African Episcopal Church, sent a petition to the U.S. Congress and President John Adams. The document was signed by seventy-three subscribers and protested the Fugitive Slave Law of 1793. Jones and his fellow signers declared,

> We cannot be insensible of the condition of our afflicted brethren, suffering under various circumstances, in different parts of the states . . . according to the design of the present Constitution formed by the General Convention, and ratified by the different states, as set forth in the preamble thereto in the following words, viz. "We the people of the United States, in order to form a more perfect union, establish justice, insure domestic tranquility, provide for the common defense, and secure the blessings of liberty to ourselves and our posterity, do ordain, &c." We apprehend this solemn compact is violated.[16]

Jones, like Allen a former slave, was incensed by the fact that earlier that year, several free black Philadelphians had been abducted and impressed into slavery. Jones could not ignore the hypocrisy of the American promise, writing, "And how increasingly is the evil aggravated, when practiced in a land high in profession of the benign doctrines of our Blessed Lord, who taught his followers to do unto others as they would they should do unto them."[17] Allen had personal experience with the gap between American republican rhetoric and practice: sometime between 1776 and 1780—at the same time that the Continental Congress was declaring that "all men are created equal" and that "they are endowed by their Creator with certain unalienable Rights, that among these are Life, Liberty and the pursuit of Happiness"—his former master, Stokeley Sturgis, sold Allen's mother and three younger siblings.[18] At this time of tremendous loss and grief, Allen, then in his late teens, was "awakened and brought to see myself poor, wretched and undone, and without the mercy of God must be lost."[19] The shock of the sudden separation from his mother, with whom he had lived his entire life, likely precipitated such feelings of desolation and ultimately Allen's conversion, with which he opens his autobiography.

Allen's autobiography reflects the profound changes taking place in American culture as a whole as well as in the emerging African American culture. Growing up during a time of great upheaval and certainly exposed to some degree to the new ideals regarding rights, freedom, and representation that British Americans were debating, Allen likely internalized these various concepts and outlooks. No longer content blindly to follow the demands of rulers with questionable divine authority and angry about excessive trade regulations and taxations, the American revolutionary thinkers embarked on a cultural as well as political revolution, resisting laws and cultural practices they thought limiting. Separation from oppression rather than reform of previous dominant cultural practices became a necessity and sovereignty a right when those governed felt overburdened by their government. Thomas Hobbes's *Leviathan* was being contested, and the justification for the social contract he envisioned revised to give the parts more influence over the whole or the right to strike out on their own when abused. The members of the revolutionary generation redefined the social order and the concept of a nation and questioned the idea that a healthy society required the tyranny of a monarch. This radical cultural revision represented an offspring not only of the Enlightenment but also of control of capital, including human capital. African Methodism became a significant element of the process of cultural renegotiation, helping to create and organize the identity of the truly oppressed group of people from which Allen emerged.

Culture as used in this study is an active process rather than a static entity or state of being. In the seventeenth century, " 'Culture' . . . means an activity, and it was a long time before the word came to denote an entity." [20] *Nature,* by contrast, is the raw material from and through which culture is made. In an effort to collapse the binary distinction between the two, Terry Eagleton has suggested that "if nature is always in some sense cultural, then cultures are built out of the ceaseless traffic with nature which we call labour." [21] The title of Allen's autobiography indicates this understanding of the relationship between culture and labor, as he is not just the passive subject of "Life" and "Experience" but also wishes to recount his "Gospel Labours," which contributed significantly to the "Rise and Progress of the African Methodist Episcopal Church in the United States of America," as the book is subtitled. Allen is well aware of his place in history, and his autobiography becomes an artifact, a product of a living and developing process of African American culture existing in large part because of the labors of people such as himself. Ironically, however, much of what constitutes Anglo-American culture also results from the unrecognized labor of Africans and African Americans who began their lives as slaves. Allen, therefore, reclaims his labor as a Methodist minister of the Gospel and one of the founders of new institutions that contribute to the development of a distinct and vibrant African American culture. Consequently, informed by the life experiences and history of its founders, the products of Allen's labors would work against oppressive practices such as slavery, the "bitter pill" of his youth, and the oppression and bigotry that led him and many other black Philadelphians to see "the necessity of erecting a place of worship for the coloured people." [22]

Like his poet predecessors Phillis Wheatley, Jupiter Hammon, and Prince Hall, Allen was born into slavery, but he eventually bought his freedom and then played an active role in further transforming the Calvinist Methodism that African Americans were receiving through British-American evangelism. Central to his efforts was the process of establishing separate places of worship and community, away from the debilitating influence of bigotry and oppression. Unlike Hammon, Allen did not believe that God had ordained slavery; rather, according to Allen, it was a sin that ought to be actively undermined by constant appeals to Christian doctrine. When the AME Church adopted its *Doctrine and Discipline* from the American Methodist Episcopal Conference in 1816, it restored a provision that slaveholders could not be members of the church, which the conference had abandoned in 1804. Allen was also cognizant of the difficulties encountered by free American blacks, and he realized that to deal with bigotry's effects on the individual, members of the black community would have to develop and lead their own institutions and carefully ally with sympathetic whites who could help gather support in the larger community as well as through the courts. Allen's work was both theological and pragmatic. Experience as a slave and then as an itinerant minister traveling with prominent Methodist clergymen taught him the power to be gained by association with strong institutions, and this knowledge allowed him to contribute significantly to emerging African American culture and to build organizations that would further challenge the contradictions of American society and politics.

Since the autobiography was published two years after Allen's death, the publishers likely were responsible for the tribute to Allen on the cover stating, "Mark the perfect man, and behold the upright: for the end of that man is peace.—Ps. xxxvii.37." Modesty—or at least the conventional modesty of the late eighteenth century—would have prevented Richard Allen from placing such an admiring epitaph on his book, but the publishers connected Allen, his labors, and his place in religious history. Allen's publishers sought to place him within the boundaries of a biblical tradition. In fact, by implying that Allen was the "perfect man," the publishers were comparing him to the David of Deuteronomic history, the founder and ruler of Jerusalem of whom chapter 37 of the Psalms speaks, the ruler of a kingdom marked by peace, prosperity, endurance, and faithfulness to God.[23] In addition to spreading Christianity more broadly, therefore, Allen's project was to spread a particular type of Christianity, Methodism, to African Americans in a way that would make it distinctively theirs, to create a New Jerusalem within the emerging new nation. Allen is marked as a founding figure not merely of a new organization but of a movement that also constitutes a significant part of the history of Christianity, thus lending continuity to emerging black religious culture, creating a heritage even as he and his followers worked to build new black institutions. Wheatley, Marrant, Hall, and other earlier black writers position Africa and Africans within a continuum of biblical and secular history that acknowledges their presence and contribution to world events. But whereas many black itinerant and slave ministers, including Marrant and David Margate, were associated with Moses and African peoples assumed the identity of the new Israelites struggling under the lash of Egyptian gloom, Allen is likened to King David, a powerful association that could only occur at this point in history, when black evangelicalism was transforming from a wilderness religion of wandering priests to a society with a tangible, material presence and national leaders. Moses may have been the lawgiver who led Israel out of Egyptian bondage, but David was the humble sheepherder who became king and finally made Israel an independent state. David Walker, the infamous black writer of the jeremiad *Appeal to the Coloured Citizens of the World*, also recognizes Allen as worthy of a place in history alongside other Christian pioneers, as having

> overcome the combined powers of devils and wicked men[. Allen] has under God planted a Church among us which will be as durable as the foundation of the earth on which it stands. Richard Allen! O my God!! The bare recollection of the labours of this man, and his ministers, among the deplorably wretched brethren . . . to bring them the knowledge of the God of Heaven, fills my soul with all those very high emotions which would take the pen of an Addison to portray. . . . When the Lord shall raise up coloured historians in succeeding generations, to present the crimes of this nation, to the gazing world, the Holy Ghost will make them do justice to the name of Bishop Allen, of Philadelphia. . . . See him and his ministers in the States of New York, New Jersey, Pennsylvania, Delaware and Maryland, carrying the gladsome tidings of free and full salvation to the coloured people.[24]

Walker's words are not mere hyperbole but recognition of Allen's contribution to the shaping of an African American institution of national stature and influence.

The epitaph on the cover of Allen's book indicates that African peoples living in America participated actively in the heritage of Christian history and culture. Allen is representative of this group, and his life, as presented in his autobiography, operates as an example and a testament to those who would follow. Allen was conscious that he was creating a new institution with far-reaching influence that could "preserve" African Americans "from the spiritual despotism which we have recently experienced." As the title of his autobiography indicates, Allen is not content with a Christianity of spiritual pacifism but advocates Christian "labour," "mutual strivings" that mean that works necessarily follow faith and grace, "as a cause does its effects."[25]

Much of what we know about Allen's early life comes from the autobiography. Allen writes in the preface that this account of his life came into being because he had been "earnestly solicited by many of my friends to leave a small detail of my life and proceedings . . . for the satisfaction of those who (after I am dead and in the grave) may feel an inclination to learn the commencement of my life."[26] Allen's autobiography is the first part of a larger work containing a supplement to the "articles of association" outlining the legal standing of Bethel Church of

Philadelphia and an account of the yellow fever epidemic of 1793. The text also contains three short addresses, "to those who keep slaves," "To The People of Colour," and "to the friends of him who hath no helper." These various texts published together, while certainly autobiographical, chronicle the establishment and growth of the AME Church and its position on slavery and bigotry. The book as a whole is a biography of the church, which is closely identified with the stages of the life of its founder.

As was conventional for early black autobiographies, Allen begins with the date and circumstances of his birth: "I was born in the year of our Lord 1760, on February 14th, a slave to Benjamin Chew of Philadelphia."[27] Allen grew up in Delaware after his first master had sold him and his mother, father, and three older siblings soon after his birth. While a slave in Delaware, Allen developed a growing consciousness of Christianity and eventually found spiritual redemption. After his "awakening," Allen began exhorting his old companions and "went rejoicing for several days, and was happy in the lord, in conversing with many old experienced Christians." But not long thereafter, Allen fell into despair because he was "brought under doubts, and was tempted to believe I was deceived." Allen was "constrained to seek the Lord afresh," and after much spiritual suffering and prayer again found his faith, never again to lose it. Allen's conversion experience did not include selecting or joining a Christian denomination, although he eventually joined the local Methodist society, which met "in the forest" near his home in Delaware.[28]

This account of his conversion experience is only one paragraph long. Allen then shifts his focus to describe his life as a slave and his lengthy efforts to buy his freedom. Although he states that he had "what the world called a good master," he lived in constant fear of being sold to a less benevolent owner. "I had it often impressed on my mind that I should one day enjoy my freedom; for slavery is a bitter pill." Moreover, he and his brother "often thought that after our master's death we were liable to be sold to the highest bidder, as [our master] was much in debt."[29] After his mother and three siblings were sold, "my troubles were increased, and I was often brought to weep between the porch and the altar." He and his brother worked harder than was required, cultivating their master's crops rather than going to church in hopes of increasing their value and avoiding being sold. According to Allen, "At length our master said he was convinced that religion made slaves better and not worse, and often boasted of his slaves for their honesty and industry."[30] Allen's master failed to realize, however, that his slaves' industry resulted not from loyalty but their sense of self-preservation and desire for stability. Allen's master eventually consented to have Methodist ministers come to preach at his house; one of them was Freeborn Garrison, who had freed his own slaves out of conscience. After hearing

Garrison's sermon, Allen's master found that "he could not be satisfied to hold slaves, believing it to be wrong." He then proposed that Allen and his brother buy their freedom: when they accumulated "sixty pounds gold and silver, or two thousand dollars continental money," they had their liberty.[31]

Allen spent the next few years cutting cordwood, working in a brickyard, and hauling salt during the Revolutionary War. At the end of the conflict, Allen began traveling extensively as an itinerant minister, joining other prominent Methodist ministers, including Benjamin Abbot, who later took over Phillips Academy in Exeter, New Hampshire, and Richard Whatcoat, whom John Wesley ordained a bishop of the Methodist Episcopal Church in 1800. Allen fondly remembered his mentors, saying of Abbot, "He was as a friend and father to me." Of Whatcoat, Allen similarly recalled, "I found a great strength traveling with him—a father of Israel. In his advice he was fatherly and friendly. He was of a mild and serene disposition." In 1785, Bishop Asbury of the newly formed Methodist Episcopal Church of America asked Allen to travel with him in the Carolinas and other southern slave territories. It is quite likely that Whatcoat, with whom Allen was traveling that year, introduced Allen to Asbury. At the first Methodist General Conference, called by John Wesley in December 1784 to formally separate American Methodism from the Church of England by creating the new Methodist Episcopal denomination, Thomas Coke ordained Asbury a bishop, and his invitation signaled an opportunity for Allen to associate and learn further from the higher echelons of the new order. Concerns regarding his health and safety led Allen to turn down Asbury's request, although the two men appear to have maintained a friendship, since Asbury later played a significant role in helping Allen form the African Methodists.

In his autobiography, Allen voices some skepticism regarding the new Methodist Episcopal denomination. He attended the 1784 Methodist General Conference, which served as a model for the first African Methodist Episcopal Conference, called by Allen and other black church leaders in April 1816. But Allen wrote less than enthusiastically about the 1784 conference: "Many of the ministers were set apart in holy orders at this Conference, and were said to be entitled to the gown; I have thought religion has been declining in the church ever since."[32] The new Methodist Episcopal Church took a strong stand against slavery, denying slave owners church membership. Nevertheless, Allen likely was disappointed when the General Conference made compromises on slavery early in the 1800s, and this disappointment likely colored his recollections of the church's founding. The betrayal of the principles of equality that defined Methodism through the eighteenth century and the general hostility that mainstream Methodism extended to black congregations eventually led to the African Methodists' separation from the General Conference.

After his arrival in Philadelphia and his assignment to St. George's Church, Allen was preaching at several different locations in the city when he "soon saw a large field open in seeking and instructing my African brethren, who had been a long forgotten people."[33] By the end of 1775, his black congregation had grown to forty-two members, and he decided to propose the idea of building a separate church. He encountered substantial resistance not only from a white Methodist clergy jealously guarding its power and influence but also from many black Philadelphians. The resistance from the white ministers can be understood as part of their effort to maintain authority over what they saw as a rapidly expanding constituency. According to Rush, Philadelphia's free black population totaled "near 3,000 souls" in 1791; nineteen years later, he wrote that a recent census had indicated that the number had surpassed 12,000.[34] Allen offers no explanation of why Philadelphia's blacks opposed the building of a separate church in 1786, but Walker indicates that fear led many free blacks to undermine efforts to improve their conditions: "I am persuaded that many of my brethren, particularly those who are ignorantly in league with slaveholders or tyrants, who acquire their daily bread by the blood and sweat of their more ignorant brethren . . . will perhaps use more abject subtlety, by affirming that this work is not worth pursuing, that we are well situated, and that there is no use in trying to better our condition, for we cannot."[35] Allen may have encountered this type of apathy, but he clearly did not allow it to end his quest. His experience as an itinerant minister, his connections within the General Conference, and his skill at networking ultimately enabled him to achieve his goal.

Raising money to buy lots and build a church was slow and difficult. By the fall of 1792, after the walkout at St. George's, Allen had become desperate to find funding. Even before the walkout, the congregation had been moving from location to location, borrowing or renting rooms in which to hold services, but the walkout left the black congregants with no place to hold regular worship. At this point, Absalom Jones and William Gray, both officers of the Free African Society, went to Benjamin Rush for help with their difficulty, and Rush arranged for them to meet with his friend, John Nicholson, the comptroller general of Pennsylvania and a successful land speculator. Rush's letter of introduction told Nicholson, "You *will* not—you *cannot* refuse their request."[36] Jones and Gray requested a loan sufficient to begin construction of the superstructure of the African church, and eight months later, in August 1793, the Free African Society received the loan. On August 22, the roof of the African Church of Philadelphia was raised and construction began in earnest.[37]

Nicholson's loan and the initiation of construction of the church could not have happened at a more crucial time. Philadelphia experienced a yellow fever outbreak in 1793, no doubt in part because of the city's rapid growth. By the beginning of September, wealthier residents had begun to flee the city, and there were not enough doctors and nurses to tend to the sick and bury the dead. Citizens willing to do so demanded exorbitant fees. Hundreds of people died each day. The epidemic may indirectly have contributed to the success of Allen's group in building its church: city officials asked black Philadelphians to aid the sick, providing a chance for the Free African Society and the rest of the black community to display their unity and effectiveness.[38] According to Allen and Jones's *A Narrative of the Proceedings of the Black People during the Late Awful Calamity in Philadelphia* (1794), "Early in September, a solicitation appeared in the public papers, to the people of colour, to come forward and assist in the distressed, perishing, and neglected sick; with a kind of assurance, that people of our colour were not liable to take the infection."[39] Rush, Philadelphia's preeminent physician, had taken out this ad after observing that no African Americans had died of the illness and concluding that they were immune to yellow fever.[40] The members of the Free African Society met with Philadelphia mayor Matthew Clarkson to discuss how they could help.

By the end of September, however, Rush realized that he had been wrong: black people were, after all, susceptible to yellow fever. Allen fell ill on September 25, causing Rush to lament, "The Negroes are everywhere submitting to the disorder. Allen, who has led their van, is very ill. If the disorder should continue to spread among them, then will the measure of our sufferings be full."[41] Rush too succumbed, but even as he lay ill in bed, he continued to write letters advocating the construction of the African church. Both Allen and Rush recovered, and Rush subsequently taught Allen and Jones how to bleed patients, in accordance with prevailing medical practices of the day.

Historian Matthew Carey soon published an account of the fever in which he disparaged the blacks' assistance to the city during the epidemic. Rush sprang to the defense of the volunteers, noting, "The merit of the blacks in their attendance upon the sick is enhanced by their not being exempt from the disorder."[42] On January 7, 1794, after the epidemic had begun to subside, Mayor Clarkson wrote a public letter of approval of the work of Allen, Jones, and their colleagues: "Having, during the prevalence of the late malignant disorder, had almost daily opportunities of seeing the conduct of Absalom Jones and Richard Allen, and the people employed by them to bury the dead—I with cheerfulness give this testimony of my approbation of their proceedings, so far as they came under my notice. Their diligence, attention, and decency of deportment, afforded me, at the time, much satisfaction."[43] To further counteract the damage done by Carey's accusations, Allen and Jones wrote their narrative of the yellow fever, which was published early in 1794. By highlighting their service to the city, this account, combined with the fact that they had risked their lives to comfort and cure the ill, helped them to continue gaining public support for first the African church and later Bethel.

The African church was finally completed and dedicated in July 1794. By the end of the spring, however, Allen had excused himself from the project and begun planning to build yet another church. Philadelphia's Methodist ministers had refused to preach for the black congregation through 1793, and its members had consequently voted to align with the Episcopal Church, which had been more accommodating toward African Americans.[44] Allen was too committed to Methodism to convert, so he exempted himself and joined with other like-minded individuals to plan another church on a plot of land he had bought several years earlier with the intention of erecting a church there.

At the dedication ceremony for the African church, held on July 17, 1794, the white rector of St. Paul's Episcopal Church, Samuel Magaw, delivered a condescending and paternalistic sermon. Magaw and many other Philadelphians, including the established clergy, found it difficult to overcome their prejudices, even in the wake of the African Americans' service during the yellow fever epidemic. "From the words thus opened and explained," Magaw began, "there arise certain duties, which you are expressly concerned in. Allow me with affectionate plainness to state and recommend them."[45] Magaw then went on to explain that the black congregation should be grateful to God "for having directed, in his own wise Providence, that you should come from a pagan darkness, to a land of Gospel light." Although he was preaching in the African church to an audience that included many members of the Free African Society, Magaw apparently saw no problem with denigrating Africa. He absolved slave traders and slaveholders from culpability by reminding the congregation, "One may say of them . . . as Joseph said to his brethren, 'But as for you, ye thought evil against us; but God meant good, to bring to pass, as it is this day, to save much people alive.'"[46] Magaw characterized slavery as part of God's benevolent plan to deliver Africans from the death of eternal damnation, contending that even those Africans and their descendants still in bondage "have received mercies enow to thank God for. His dispensations are unquestionably wise and proper. Whatever he permits, will turn to the real profit of such as do resign themselves to his good pleasure. Your Present situation does not hinder you from being Christ's freemen."[47] Magaw's theology suggests the legitimacy of the old proslavery argument that God is the sole sovereign of the universe, dictating the events of the world, and that humans must submit to his will. While certainly consistent with orthodox Calvinism, this theology also supports the political status quo politic. Magaw is telling the African church's congregation to turn a blind eye to their suffering and that of others and to embrace subservience, to "resign themselves to [God's] good pleasure"—humility and subservience to white masters and authority. Although Philadelphia's Methodists had been paternalistic, the denomination's theology and international position opposed such ideas, and Magaw's pronouncements must have surprised those celebrating the opening of Philadelphia's first black church.

Magaw then reminded the congregants that their next duty is to be grateful to "your earthly benefactors, who planned your emancipation from slavery . . . whose labors were unwearied on your behalf."[48] Magaw further told the congregation to remember Benjamin Franklin, the Pennsylvania Society for the Abolition of Slavery, and especially the citizens of Philadelphia, who had assisted "in the building of this handsome, spacious, and very convenient church."[49] Magaw never mentioned the efforts of the leaders of the Free African Society or any of the black Philadelphians who had worked to help African Americans secure and maintain their freedom. For Magaw, only whites warranted gratitude for aiding the members of the African church. The sermon never mentioned whites' appreciation of African Americans' help in fighting the yellow fever epidemic that had ravaged the city less than a year before.

Magaw next lectured the congregation on the importance of maintaining humility and avoiding pride, of which he had heard "there is a great deal . . . among your people, already; and that it is increasing extremely fast."[50] Magaw and other ministers must have been alarmed by the happiness and celebratory spirit that had accompanied African Americans' recent successes in securing funding, building the African church, helping to fight the yellow fever epidemic, and starting schools. After commenting on the debt owed to whites for extirpating blacks from slavery and paganism, he built on this base with advice that was stern and intentionally demeaning: "When you are tempted to cherish the least pride, in your freedom—in dress—in your favorable reception among your fellow-citizens, and even in this stately building; or in any of your civil, as well as religious privileges; then check yourselves, by confessing privately and publicly, that 'a slave ready to perish, was my father.' "[51] Even more ominously, Magaw warned the black congregation to be circumspect, to "remember that you have enemies, as well as friends; that you will be narrowly watched; and that less allowance will be made for your failings, than those of other people."[52] Magaw concluded the sermon with a message to those members of the church who were not free: "It is a dispensation of Providence, as I hinted already, to which you should submit in quietness, for conscience sake: and in so doing, you shall certainly meet with good."[53] Magaw opened and closed with a message of submission to slavery as the will of God. Rather than directing righteous indignation at slavery or oppression, the minister chastised the black church members for pride and reminded them to be grateful for white Philadelphians' help. The members of the African church's congregation, at first excited about this inaugural day, must have felt disappointment at hearing a scolding and anticlimactic sermon by a clergyman they had trusted to represent them well as Episcopalians.

One of the problems that enabled and possibly compelled Magaw's sermon was the Episcopal Church's adamant refusal to make slavery a matter of discipline.[54] Church leaders wanted to avoid any discussion of the politics of slavery and consequently took a position of neutrality, calling human bondage both an evil committed by men and the will of God and therefore the source of some good. Magaw was probably very aware of the activities of the Free African Society, one of which was providing freed slaves with copies of the necessary paperwork to ensure that they could not be forced back into slavery. The *Narrative of the Proceedings of the Black People* contained "An Address to Those Who Keep Slaves and Uphold the Practice" in which Jones and Allen clearly condemn slavery as not only unjust but unholy: "We do not wish to make you angry, but excite your attention to consider, how hateful slavery is in the sight of that God, who hath destroyed kings and princes, for their oppression of the poor slaves; Pharaoh and his princes with the posterity of King Saul, were destroyed by the protector and avenger of slaves."[55] Jones and Allen also rebuke the contention that slaves are content or should be content with their condition, offering a caution about the consequences of unchecked slavery: "The dreadful insurrections [slaves] have made, when opportunity has offered, is enough to convince a reasonable man, that great uneasiness and not contentment, is the inhabitant of their hearts."[56] Magaw was also likely responding to Jones's connections to Rush, an outspoken supporter of abolition. Magaw did not want Rush and others' political efforts to serve a message to the church and its members to become involved in the controversy. Magaw's message was one of passivity, but Jones, soon to be ordained an Episcopal minister, was anything but passive in his ecclesiastical and political work.

Jones moved to deal with Magaw's message of submission and gratitude, drafting a resolution explaining "The Causes and Motives for Establishing St. Thomas's African Church of Philadelphia." Jones casts the work of establishing the church as occurring not only out of a sense of humility and service to God but also out of a desire to "organize ourselves for the purpose of promoting the health the people all, but more particularly our relatives, of color."[57] Jones makes clear both that African Americans were actively engaged in the development of the church and that they had, "after many consultations, and some years of deliberation thereon, . . . gone forward to erect a house for the glory of God, and our mutual advantage to meet in for clarification and social religious worship."[58] Jones wanted to ensure that the congregation as well as Episcopal authorities knew that much thought and work had gone into the construction and organization of the African church. Jones's address constitutes not just a response to Magaw's sermon but a formal dedication signed by the church's black founders and trustees. In the document, they "RESOLVE AND DECREE, To resign and conform ourselves to the Protestant Episcopal Church of North America. . . . To be henceforward known and called by the name and title of St. Thomas's African Episcopal Church of Philadelphia, to be governed by us and our successors for ever."[59] Thus, the church's founders formally dedicated St. Thomas's on August 12, 1794.

Allen might seem to have fallen from the scene at this point, but this was not the case. Far from dissuaded from his desire to open a black Methodist church, Allen redoubled his efforts. A year earlier, Allen had bought a lot at Lombard and Sixth Streets, intending it to be the site of the proposed African church. However, the trustees found a Fifth Street lot more desirable, and St. Thomas's African Church was constructed there. When the rest of the committee instructed Allen to give up the lot, he decided that he "would sooner keep it myself," perhaps already aware that the African Society might resist Methodism.[60] On May 5, 1794, Allen and eleven other black Methodists met to plan an African Methodist church.[61] The group bought an old frame building that had been a blacksmith's shop and had it pulled by horses to the new site. A few weeks later, in July, Bishop Asbury visited Philadelphia, and Allen asked his old acquaintance to open the church. Asbury dedicated the Bethel African Church, with the name suggested by John Dickins, a minister at St. George's Methodist Church who also attended the opening, during prayer. Unlike the opening of St. Thomas's African Church, with Magaw's dour sermon, Bethel's dedication featured high spirits: wrote Allen, "My dear Lord was with us, so that there was many hearty Amen's echoed through the house."[62] Allen's dream had finally reached fruition.

By all accounts, Bethel's opening represented the final occasion on which a minister from St. George's attended the new church without conflict arising. According to Allen, after the dedication, "our warfare and troubles now began afresh." For several years thereafter, various St. George's elders troubled Bethel with jurisdictional disputes and attempts to take control of the church and its property. Allen and his congregation initially did not intend to join the Methodist conference but found that if they did not do so, they could not receive church legacies that had been left for them. The incorporation papers were drawn up by a church official who assigned all of Bethel's church property to the white conference, leaving Allen and his trustees without legal proprietorship over their own church. They remained at the mercy of Bethel's elders, the same officials who had prompted the walkout from St. George's and who had been hostile to the formation of a black church. In 1807, church leaders found a legal loophole, and the articles of incorporation were amended so that the black congregation gained authority and control of its property. Incensed, the elders at St. George's continued to pressure Bethel, contending that the amendment was not legally binding. One elder ultimately sued for control of Bethel, and after a long legal battle, the Pennsylvania Supreme Court ruled in favor of the Bethel congregation.[63] Once again, Bethel was independent and under the control of its founders.

Bethel's success occasioned celebration among black Methodist congregations across the United States. The Bethel Church of Baltimore was embroiled in a similar legal battle, and on January 21, 1816, the minister of that congregation, Daniel Coker, preached a celebratory sermon comparing the Philadelphians' victory to the return of the Jews from captivity in Babylon.[64] News of Coker's legal battle as well as of other problems encountered by other black Methodist churches convinced Allen to call a general meeting of church leaders to discuss their common problems. In April 1816, leaders representing congregations from several states assembled in Philadelphia and decided to "become one body, under the name of the African Methodist Episcopal Church."[65] During the conference, Allen was called away on personal business. When he returned, he found that the delegates had elected him bishop of the new AME Church. Allen, who had held no official church office higher than deacon, now found himself the head of a new denomination of national scope. On April 11, five ordained ministers, including his old friend, Jones, consecrated Allen bishop of the AME Church. Jones had been ordained a minister of the Episcopal Church and an elder of St. Thomas's African Episcopal Church, and now he was present to confirm Allen as the leader of the largest church body of African Americans ever organized. Allen's dreams as an unlicensed itinerant minister for a small congregation of black Philadelphians thirty years earlier had grown into a movement that created the most powerful black institution in the United States and that contributed to the advancement of African American educational, social, and political rights.

In his autobiography, Allen represents his life experiences and labors as a Christian life in progress, and he comes to embody the "perfect man" of Psalms 37:37. By the end of his autobiography, Allen is transformed into a David figure, a humble sheepherder (or in Allen's case, a slave) who becomes the leader of a people. Allen as well as his friends and followers, including Jones, Coker, Cyrus Bustill, David Walker, Maria Stewart, and innumerable others, used his example of leadership through Christian principles to further develop a social theology with which to wage an activist war against oppression that legal and ecclesiastical authorities could not ignore. This social theology, based on the pioneering work of the authors discussed in earlier chapters of this volume, resonates throughout nineteenth-century pamphlets, newspapers, and books. The writers of these works recalled their debts to their predecessors and sought to promulgate the generative potential of African American theologies founded on cultural and social as well as spiritual responsibility.

CHAPTER SIX

Maria Stewart and the Mission of Black Women in Evangelicalism

As this book demonstrates, beginning with the chapter on Jupiter Hammon, late-eighteenth- and early-nineteenth-century blacks adopted a range of intellectual positions concerning the proper theological schools of thought related to slavery and human rights. And while Phillis Wheatley, Hammon's contemporary, was in many ways his complete intellectual and theological opposite, her concerns were broad enough to address rights on the level of a universal humanity. In fact, most of the writers examined thus far, to one degree or another, couch their ideals in universalizing language. The tendency can be misleading, as most "universal" claims tend to leave out some subjects. In this case, the universalizing tendency translates to civil rights as they apply to the interests of men—not women.[1] However, Maria Stewart further expands the discussions of the struggles against black oppression when she addresses African Americans on the topic of gender inequality as relevant to racial inequality.

Gender inequality colluded with racial oppression to create a double bind for African Americans. Even as many African-descended peoples struggled against the institutionalized racism and systemic intellectualizing of oppression that proposed just cause for a permanent black underclass as well as slavery (intellectualizing that many blacks accepted, seeking some sort of spiritual comfort to explain what appeared to be the will of a seemingly apathetic God), gender inequality stood as a barrier to true, fundamental human equality as long as black men and women imagined each other on different levels of human worth and dignity. This is not to say that widespread, open antipathy existed between black men and women but to acknowledge that gender inequalities affected African American efforts to bring about positive social change and hampered the progress of the movement toward social equality. In fact, hostility toward the idea of an outspoken black woman leader eventually led Stewart to abandon her call for active political struggle against white oppression. Her efforts to guide black Americans to deal with the matter of gender bias and lack of moral cohesion as a people, which she believed to be a necessary precondition for universal social justice, was muted as she left the public arena as a speaker and writer, most likely as a result of mounting hostility toward her Boston-based efforts.

Stewart fashioned for herself a public identity as a prophet. She believed herself to be chosen and empowered by God—specifically, to speak out against the transgressions of both black and white Christians who she believed had abandoned biblical foundations for the moral and ethical structure of the newly emergent American society. Although she never uses the word *prophet* to describe herself, she announces that God has charged her with stating the errors of the society around her and placed within her the authority to speak on his behalf. Her career as a speaker and writer focused on the experiential relationship between God and humanity, but Stewart also eventually sought to reveal that pietism assumed equality between the sexes and that women were just as endowed as men with the capacity to expound on matters of theodicy as well as to provide spiritual direction and leadership within a traditionally androcentric milieu.

In her first published work, "Religion and the Pure Principles of Morality," Stewart tells her readers some of her background, both legitimizing her claim to be a Christian touched directly by the irresistible presence of a redeeming deity and allowing herself the right to speak as a Christian for Christians. Stewart tells her readers that she "was left an orphan at five years of age" and was "bound out in a clergyman's family." She continues, "[I] was left a widow in 1829; was, as I humbly hope and trust, brought to the knowledge of the truth. . . . [F]rom the moment I experienced the change, I felt a strong desire, with the help and assistance of God, to devote the remainder of my days to piety and virtue. . . . I would willingly sacrifice my life for the cause of God and my brethren."[2] This testimony introduces the reader to a person beset by tragedies and trials throughout her life, a life of suffering in which she received hope and direction from God's divine influence. Stewart establishes for herself the ethos of someone who has endured sufferings, making the miracle of her redemption that much greater. Rather than establishing the narrative of a sinner, as in most spiritual autobiographies, from Sts. Paul and Augustine to Jonathan Edwards and John Marrant, Stewart tells a different origin tale to establish her credibility as a Christian saint. While Marrant and most previous spiritual autobiographers focus on the conversion process as a progression from sin to salvation, Stewart's brief narrative moves from suffering to salvation. She does not implicate herself in any great personal error, but as she makes clear throughout her writing career, the origin of suffering is sin—specifically, the collective sinfulness of African Americans, who she argues have abandoned God and consequently will continue to suffer from oppression and other ills. Her personal sufferings have prepared her for her true calling, that of a prophet.

Suffering is as much a part of the human experience as sin, and Stewart links the two in her essays and speeches, as do the Old Testament prophets, to establish her ethos of prophetic suffering. The information that she had been bound out to a clergyman's family established on a rhetorical level the fact that she had been exposed during her youth to a religious atmosphere. Her association with such a family also should have afforded her a degree of education that might not otherwise have been available to an orphan. But although she lived in a religious household in which "the seeds of piety and virtue" were sown in her mind, she was "deprived of the advantages of education, though my soul thirsted for knowledge."[3] The experience definitely exposed Stewart to the idea that learning was important, an ideal that would become a clarion call throughout her speeches and essays. Thus, the tragedies of losing her parents, being denied education within a Christian home, and then being widowed so early in life mark her as having experienced suffering with which her audience can identify as part of the human experience.[4] This prophetic suffering not only connects Stewart and her audience but also sets her up as a spiritual vessel for the dispensation of God's will.

The second movement in this brief autobiographical account is the conversion experience, an event that led her not only to turn toward God but to pledge to do his will until her death. Such pledges are not unusual in spiritual autobiography, part of the Christian life in progress includes the process of birth, sin, suffering, and conversion.[5] However, she pledges herself not just to the will of God but to the service of her "brethren."[6] She uses *brethren* not as a generalized term for fellow Christians but to refer to Africans and African Americans who have also suffered as a result of sin. This is a unique movement in the expression of a pledge to exercise God's virtues. Rather than maintaining a purely personal obligation to observe the duties of the Christian life, Stewart takes on a mission that involves the resuscitation of African Americans' portion of the covenant with God. She clarifies, "All the nations of the earth are crying out for liberty and equality. Away, away with tyranny and oppression! And shall Afric's sons be silent any longer?"[7] The essay contains little in the way of further autobiographical detail, as Stewart focuses mainly on the twin issues of sin and suffering as a result of moral neglect. However, the essay gives one more hint of what would become a persistent problem in Stewart's ministry, the problem of gender bias. Even as Stewart elucidates a corporate solution to black suffering through social and cultural unification under a common system of morality and virtues, she states, "I am sensible of former prejudices; but it is time for prejudices and animosities to cease from among us. I am sensible of exposing myself to calumny and reproach. . . . O ye daughters of Africa, awake! Awake! Arise! No longer sleep nor slumber, but distinguish yourselves."[8] Stewart warns readers about the effects of gender bias and encourages black women to take an active role in public life. As she notes, she is aware that she would traditionally encounter criticism for speaking out publicly, but this, too, is in line with her role as a contemporary prophet.

Like the biblical prophets, Stewart gives little account of her life in her early writings. Unlike the spiritual autobiography, the details of the prophet's life are mostly irrelevant, as the prophetic writer seeks to account for the future, punishment, and/or eventual regeneration of the people chosen by God.[9] Isaiah, Jeremiah, Ezekiel, and Amos, for example, all briefly mention their calling to the role of prophet and give short accounts of their backgrounds, but the narrative focuses not on the individual prophet but on the state, fate, and regeneration of the people or nation as a whole. For Stewart, that meant a general moral reawakening, which included an ethics of self-determination as well as a recognition that black women were active participants in God's plans rather than passive objects meant to sit by silently. Stewart genuinely believed that she was called to the station of prophet, and she took seriously her appointed role as God's mouthpiece, modeling her public persona according to the types familiar from the Bible. Her stance as a prophetic leader, particularly one who was a woman, positioned her to expand the discussion of universal rights for black people that also recognize women as authoritative leadership figures.

According to the theology inherent in Stewart's early writings, authority to speak on social as well as biblical matters issues from God. Reticent at the beginning of her ministry, Stewart states in "Religion and the Pure Principles of Morality," "I am sensible of my ignorance; but such knowledge as God has given to me, I impart to you."[10] Her statement is not a general recognition of pietism, or the one-on-one experiential relationship with God that had become a cornerstone of African American religion by the early nineteenth century, but a statement of her peculiar relationship with divinity. Stewart speaks as a special agent of God, as a latter-day prophet, and her boldness quickly increases as she develops as a writer and speaker on the moral component of civil rights. A few months after the publication of "Religion and the Pure Principles of Morality" and shortly after the release of her pamphlet, *Meditations from the Pen of Maria W. Stewart*, she found herself publicly defending her activities as a spiritual writer and leader. Her earlier recognition of gender bias was arguably her least damning warning against bigotry toward women engaging in public life. In *Meditations*, however, Stewart boldly proclaims that her writing "is the word of God, though men and devils may oppose it. It is the word of God; and little did I think that any of the professed followers of Christ would have frowned upon me, and discouraged and hindered its progress."[11] Stewart believes that God speaks through her and that her will and desires are irrelevant, just like the sinful tendencies of those who oppose her works on the grounds that she is a woman. As she states in "Religion and the Pure Principles of Morality," "I am but a feeble instrument."[12] Like Old Testament prophets, Stewart found that she was speaking truths strongly critiquing the people she was trying to aid, putting her in a difficult position as the harbinger of both God's wrath and the fulfillment of his covenant.

Stewart's communications with divinity imply, among other things, two important theological positions. First, she indicates that God, rather than being a distant and indifferent sovereign, is actively involved in the workings of humanity. Second, divinity remains in direct communication with his chosen representatives, who are charged with directing the people toward morality and justice. These prophets often cannot discern a rationale for God's choice but nevertheless adhere to their calling. For example, Amos of the Old Testament did not choose to become a prophet: he was not a priest but a shepherd and a grower of fruit who claimed, "I was no prophet, neither was I a prophet's son. . . . And the Lord said unto me, Go prophesy unto my people Israel."[13] Stewart recognized that in shaping and describing her station as a prophet, she had to identify with a model such as Amos rather than one of those agents of God born into the position as a priest: "Again, why the almighty hath imparted unto me the power of speaking thus, I cannot tell."[14] However, God's power and sovereignty enable him to turn people from humble beginnings into his special agents of prophesy and change. In fact, Stewart believed that it was important to recognize that the will of God operated directly on the lives of people, including women, and she asked at the end of her career at a public speaker, "Why cannot a religious spirit animate us now? Why cannot we become divines and scholars? Although learning is somewhat requisite, yet recollect that those great apostles, Peter and James, were ignorant and unlearned."[15] Just as with the Old Testament prophets and the New Testament apostles, the individual will is sublimated to that of God, and the prophet becomes an instrument through which God makes his will known. In this way, God has a direct line of communication through the human agent chosen for this special station—in this case, Stewart, a black woman living in modern times.[16]

Unlike John Marrant and David Margate, black evangelicals who likened themselves and African Americans to the Israelites in the days of Moses, delivered from Egyptian bondage, and unlike Richard Allen, whose persona and society-building efforts paralleled events in Israel in the time of King David, Stewart aligns herself and her ministry with the prophets who lament the fall of Israel into a degraded state of immorality and remoteness from God.[17] "Why-fore hast thou so long withheld from us the divine influences of thy Holy Spirit? Wherefore hast thou hardened our hearts and blinded our eyes? It is because we have honored thee with our lips, but our hearts are far from thee. We have pol-luted thy Sabbaths, and even our most holy things have been solemn mockery to thee."[18] Indeed, Stewart attempts to appropriate the voice and rationale for divine justice as Isaiah articulates it, beginning his explanation of Israel's fail-ings and the futility of the trappings of worship without recognizing the foun-dational moral principles of righteousness that inform proper social relations: "To what purpose is the multitude of your sacrifices unto me? Saith the Lord: I am full of the burnt offerings of rams, and the fat of fed beasts; and I delight not in the blood of bullocks, or of lambs, or of goats. . . . Bring me no more vain oblations; incense is an abomination to me. . . . [L]earn to do well; seek judg-ment, relieve the oppressed, judge the fatherless, plead for the widow."[19] Like Isaiah, Stewart wants to show that worship in the church and the ceremonies of Christianity are just the superficial trappings of religion if those practices do not correspond with and promote social justice.

Throughout her written works, Stewart tries to reconcile a perennial problem of Judeo-Christian philosophy—the question of how a benevolent and caring God can tolerate suffering in the world. Like Jeremiah and the other prophets who deal with this question, Stewart argues that suffering is a result of human-ity's sins, and God's punishment of those sins is just, since God, who is all-caring, must also be the dispenser of universal justice. "Righteousness exalteth a nation, but sin is a reproach to any people. Why is it, my friends, that our eyes have been blinded by ignorance, to the present moment? 'Tis on account of sin."[20] In this instance, Stewart is addressing the problem of education and access to learning, contending that black Christians, her primary audience, can owe much of their plight to the sinfulness of their actions and attitudes toward God. In this vein, Stewart aligns African peoples with the beleaguered Israelites, whose sufferings at the hands of an army of enemies result from sin: "I really think we are as wretched and miserable a state as was the house of Israel in the days of Jeremiah."[21]

Identifying African peoples at this time in history with a fallen Israel would seem like a bleak and difficult analogy; however, as all of the prophetic liter-ature of the Old Testament reminds the Israelites, they are a special people in God's eyes, and he wholly intends to keep his covenant with the chosen people, restoring the greatness of the African peoples. Stewart's prophetic condemna-tion of sin constitutes a sincere attempt to understand suffering among African peoples and to translate it into a rational theodicy consistent with her biblical upbringing. As a result, Africans are less like Israel during the Egyptian captiv-ity and exodus or during the kingdoms of Solomon and David than like Israel during its destruction and oppression by Babylon. By identifying the plight of African Americans in this way, Stewart both places African Americans within the continuum of biblical history and understands how God's chosen people, black Christians, could nevertheless suffer such terrible oppression at the hands of white Americans. Wheatley calls slaveholding Americans "our Modern Egyptians"; for Stewart, in contrast, the worldly oppressors of African-descended peoples seem more like a modern Babylon ruining Israel as documented in the books of Isaiah and Jeremiah.[22] Stewart participates in a long tradition of redefining Christian typology to aid in explaining the social present. Just as Martin Luther depicted the reign of the Catholic papacy as a type of Babylon and the Protestant movement as a type of Israel's deliverance, Stewart figures the American slaveocracy as Babylon and the oppressed African peoples as Israel.[23]

What specific complaints has God lodged against his chosen people? Stewart's charges resemble those advanced by her mentor, David Walker: African Americans have abandoned the moral principles of virtue exercised through the pursuit of knowledge and unifying practices of Christian struggle for justice. In other words, Stewart believes that black people need to wage a unified struggle for education and civil rights in the face of white oppression. Under Stewart's theology, righteousness and justice are neither abstractions nor separate from the field of human action. Justice and religion are not separate from one another, and righteousness (another word for God's justice) results from the confluence of religious observance and just relations between the members of the covenanted community.

Therefore, religious practice, as it relates to everyday lived experience, necessarily entails the just actions of members of the socioreligious group as well as observance of proper relations between worshipper and the sovereign lawgiver.[24] Stewart believed that the active pursuit of education and an aggressive pursuit of civil rights were moral duties and extensions of expected religious observances. And as Cain Hope Felder has pointed out, the Old Testament prophets inveighed against "cultic excesses and social injustices because of a recurring moral and 'religious' malaise into which the covenanted people" had fallen and "from which they needed to be extricated."[25] Likewise, Stewart saw African Americans as derelict in their pursuit of knowledge and education as well as leaving the pursuit of civil rights in the hands of white abolitionists and politicians.

Often arguing in the abstract ("Never, no, never will the chains of slavery and ignorance burst, till we become united as one, and cultivate among ourselves the pure principles of piety, morality and virtue"), Stewart prescribes more specific solutions for what she sees as the moral malaise of African Americans suffering the pangs of injustice ("Let us promote ourselves and improve our own talents").[26] Stewart further develops ideas of black self-determination as religious duty in the face of oppression. Just as Prince Hall and David Walker called for self-determination in the fields of education and economic uplift, Stewart furthers that cause as a moral obligation that must be recognized as being as much religious observance as social and cultural development: "I am of a strong opinion that the day will come when we unite, heart and soul, and turn our attention to knowledge and improvement, that day the hissing and reproach among the nations of the earth against us will cease. And even those who now point at us with the finger of scorn, will aid and befriend us. It is of no use for us to sit with our hands folded, hanging our heads like bulrushes, lamenting our wretched condition; but let us make a mighty effort, and arise; and if no one will promote or respect us, let us promote and respect ourselves."[27] In this early essay, "Religion and the Pure Principles of Morality," Stewart boldly states that the pursuit of education as a moral obligation will lead to the end of God's punishment. Women played a special part in the pursuit of moral absolution through education through their role as the caretakers and primary educators of children. The promotion of this traditional role initially does not seem out of place in a context in which the domestic and the social are divided along gender lines— women remained confined to the home, while men were encouraged to pursue the social realm. This relegation of black women to the domestic realm does not seem like a liberating or liberatory move; however, Stewart's promotion of female institution building and economic determination signals her first foray, other than the personal role of prophet, into a feminist agenda of equality in the social realm.

Stewart's petition to "let every female heart become united, and let us raise a fund ourselves; and at the end of one year and a half, we might be able to lay the corner stone for the building of a High School, that the higher branches of knowledge might be enjoyed by us," formed part of a burgeoning ideal that would lead her to recognize the worth and value of women's efforts in the pursuit of a morality based on education.[28] Stewart holds the domestic realm as the normative social space for women to inhabit socially—"Let each one strive to excel in good housewifery, knowing that prudence and economy are the road to wealth"—but in her later works, she clearly abandons the cult of domesticity for a position that argues for women's full social equality as a prerequisite for a return to righteousness and God's full approval.[29]

The tone and direction of Stewart's message as well as her gender stood in the way of widespread acceptance among her primary audience, and the attitudes of her Boston audience stood in the way of her full acceptance as a spokesperson for the cause of religion and civil rights. In the burgeoning black theologies of the middle and late eighteenth century, God connects with the individual agent directly through the conversion process; however, Stewart's writing suggests that she believes that God still needs special spokespersons to communicate his will to the masses. In this particular case, he has chosen a woman to bear the contemporary message to his chosen people. Stewart encountered difficulty negotiating this problem in the context of New Testament Christian polemics, particularly St. Paul's mandate that women stay silent on public issues. This, like Paul's ambivalence toward slavery, creates a double bind for a black Christian such as Stewart, who must negotiate doctrines seemingly at odds with both her calling as a prophet and her antislavery message of equality relying on a Christian tradition of biblical exegesis.

Long-standing cultural tradition created a general tendency against women's participation in public life, but many men probably found Stewart even more difficult to bear as a consequence of her implicit and often explicit criticism of black men's failure to stand up and challenge the authorities for the rights of black people. Regardless of whatever egos she might damage, Stewart had to speak what she believed to be the truth as revealed through divine inspiration. In the end, Stewart followed most of her black evangelical predecessors by either reinterpreting or abandoning parts of the Scriptures that seemed at odds with a theology based on equality and liberation. "St. Paul declared that it was a shame for a woman to speak in public, yet our great High Priest and Advocate did not condemn the woman for a more notorious offense than this; neither will he condemn this worthless worm." This is a bold reinterpretation of Scripture, declaring that St. Paul's pronouncements play a subordinate role to Christ's words and actions as represented in the Gospels. Stewart refers to the alleged prostitution of Mary Magdalene and contends that by forgiving Mary of her sins of the flesh and making her one of his closest followers, Christ sets a precedent for women's role in the church and in public life. She goes on to state, "Again; holy women ministered unto Christ and the Apostles; and women of refinement in all ages, more or less, have had a voice in moral, religious and political subjects," thereby further establishing a place for women in the ongoing unfolding of biblical history.[30]

Standing as boldly against St. Paul as against contemporary critics who would have her and other women remain silent and basing that conviction on Scriptures, Stewart does for women what she and other abolitionist evangelists did when they argued that slavery could not be justified by biblical precedent. In a key piece of exegesis, Stewart establishes that Christ's pronouncements in one part of the Bible take precedence over later writings, regardless of how authoritative they are. By this means, Stewart overcomes the problems of Christian arguments supporting both slavery and oppression of women. Stewart also shows that she strongly believes in the concept that biblical statutes must be read in some historical context, noting, "Did St. Paul but know of our wrongs and deprivations, I presume he would make no objection to our pleading in public for our rights."[31] Stewart believes that St. Paul would have had more flexible views about women and about slavery had he lived to understand its depredations in an American context.

In addition, Stewart also believed that the Scriptures were not the last word on God's relationship with humanity. She also believed that as part of the ongoing unfolding of a preordained biblical history, people such as herself could be spokespersons for God and have as much authority to speak on social matters as the writers of biblical texts. In Stewart's understanding of divinity, God remained active in the world, inspiring individuals to continue the work of prophesy and revelation, regardless of race or gender. In this way, the lessons that made Stewart unpopular even among those she wanted to see treated with dignity and equality also frightened many members of that group divided by gender bias.

With the rise of black institutions, former slaves and their descendants increasingly began to see themselves as leaders and authorities with a unique place in the American republic, and Stewart encouraged this viewpoint as a means toward full abolition and equality. Stewart saw organizing on a principled Christian foundation of morality and ethics as a precondition for the end of oppression. Stewart took the step, radical for the time, of assuming a leadership role in the movement for abolition and equal rights. For the first time, an African American woman assumed the mantle of a written prophet and spokesperson for her people. While black men such as John Marrant assumed prophetic status with various degrees of success, the idea of a woman with such a close one-on-one relationship with God was unusual and encountered significant resistance from precisely the group of free black Bostonians she sought to help. Stewart's calling extended beyond the communication with God expected of all Christian converts as part of the process of regeneration. Although she met with great resistance, Stewart's faith and works forced black Christians to confront not only the oppression of racialized slavery and social discrimination but also gender inequality among African Americans, which she believed had to be eliminated so that blacks could fight for their rights as a unified people. Stewart did not believe that racialized oppression could be fought without eradicating gender oppression. Unlike most of the writers examined in this study, Stewart's connection of faith with the temporal duty to fight oppression to bring into being an egalitarian Christian world extended to issues of gender as well as those of race.

NOTES

Introduction

1. Hammon, *America's First Negro Poet*, 64, lines 97–100.

2. Numerous scholars of African American history have dealt with the differences between the Christian doctrines delivered to slaves by early Calvinist missionaries and what the Calvinists themselves practiced. The missionaries did not separate the secular and the spiritual, although they expected their converted slaves to do so. See Raboteau, *Slave Religion*, 103–4. The differing doctrines that Anglican missionaries attempted to transmit to slaves is addressed later in this introduction and in chapter 1.

3. Hammon, *America's First Negro Poet*, 52, lines 65–68.

4. Darsey , *Prophetic Tradition*, 70.

5. Wheatley, *Collected Works*, 74, 177.

6. Ibid., 176.

7. Aptheker, *Negro Slave Revolts*, 10. See also Frey and Wood, *Come Shouting to Zion*.

8. W. E. B. Du Bois was the first serious scholar to study the black church, making this important observation and many others about the institution in *The Souls of Black Folk*.

9. Woodson, *History of the Negro Church*, 2nd ed.

10. Raboteau, *Slave Religion*, 67–73.

11. Ibid., 71–75.

12. This intellectual movement operated at the same time as a number of Afro-British writers was building their presence as part of an intellectual community. See Sandiford, *Measuring the Moment*.

13. Bassard suggests the narrative paradigm in which African peoples are discussed must be reconfigured so that the language does not continue to inscribe assumptions of inferiority or incapacity in enslaved Africans. Bassard instead puts forward a "language of African survivalship" that "calls to mind the survival of Africanity and African structures within New World spaces" (*Spiritual Interrogations*, 35–36). I build on that foundation, further inscribing a language of survival and triumph in the face of overwhelming inhuman oppression. This volume also moves critical attention away from recapitulations of black suffering that ultimately put the focus on the agency of white oppressors, refocusing critical attention on resistance and the successes of black intellectualism and institution building of the period in these "New World spaces."

14. Scheick, *Authority and Female Authorship*, 108.

15. Hegel, *Philosophy of History*, 93, 95.

16. As chapters 3 and 4 discuss, many of the writers of the black transatlantic reveal Africa and Africans as principal players in biblical history.

17. Patterson, *Slavery and Social Death*, 5.

18. Ibid.

19. Berlin, "From Creole to African," 19–20.

20. Morgan, *Slave Counterpoint*, 420.

21. See also Gibson, *Two Letters*; Frey and Wood, *Come Shouting to Zion*; Raboteau, *Slave Religion*.

22. John, "Construction of Racial Meaning," 47.

23. Ibid., 48.

24. Creel, *Peculiar People*, 239. The benne seed ritual involved a priest spreading seeds of various types on the ground for criminal offenders to pick up as part of a nonviolent humiliation rite. See Creel, *Peculiar People*, for more information on the nature of this practice among Gullah Baptists. While this practice may no longer exist widely in contemporary American black churches, it is a specific and very interesting example of how African peoples reinterpreted both African and European religious traditions to suit the material and psychological conditions of life in British North America.

25. Patterson, *Slavery and Social Death*, 5.

26. Frey and Wood, *Come Shouting to Zion*, 105.

27. Bassard, *Spiritual Interrogations*, 60–61.

28. Mather, *Negro Christianized*, 3.

29. Ibid.

30. Colossians 3:11 reads, "Where there is neither Greek nor Jew, circumcision nor uncircumcision, Barbarian, Scythian, bond nor free: but Christ is all, and in all."

31. Gibson, *Two Letters*, 11.

32. Ibid., 10.

33. Ibid., 11–14.

34. Creel, *Peculiar People*, 80.

35. Raboteau, *Slave Religion*, 212–13.

36. Raboteau, *Fire in the Bones*, 80.

37. Plato, *Phaedrus*, 46–49.

38. Plato, *Last Days of Socrates*, 63–64.

39. Losonsky, *Enlightenment and Action*, 3.

40. Winiarski, "Souls Filled with Ravishing Transport," 3.

41. Ibid.

42. Ibid., 29.

43. Gibson, *Observations*, 4.

44. Ibid., 7.

45. Ibid., 10.

46. Ibid.

47. Raboteau, *Slave Religion*, 67.

48. Ibid., 62.

49. Herskovits, *Myth of the Negro Past*; Raboteau, *Slave Religion*.

One. *Jupiter Hammon and the Written Beginnings of Black Theology*

1. See O'Neale, *Jupiter Hammon*; Richards, "Nationalist Themes"; Guruswamy, " 'Thou Hast the Holy Word.' " Each argues for the resistance in Hammon's writing.

I present these texts as points for comparison with my own analysis. While I disagree with these writers on the point of Hammon's resistance, their works raise important questions concerning Hammon's hermeneutics as well as the difficulties of hermeneutics in Hammon scholarship.

2. See Simpson, *Puritanism*, 50–60.

3. See Hammon, *America's First Negro Poet*, 74.

4. Ibid.

5. Ibid.

6. The Christian conception of a master-slave relationship is stated in the Pauline epistle Ephesians 6:5–9: "Servants, be obedient to them that are your masters according to the flesh, with fear and trembling, in singleness of your heart, as unto Christ; Not with eyeservice, as menpleasers; but as the servants of Christ, doing the will of God from the heart; With good will doing service, as to the Lord, and not to men: Knowing that whatsoever good thing any man doeth, the same shall he receive of the Lord, whether he be bond or free. And, ye masters, do the same things unto them, forbearing threatening: knowing that your Master also is in heaven; neither is there respect of persons with him." Apologists and proponents of slavery often quoted this passage, among others of Paul and other biblical writers, as proof of slavery's compatibility with Christianity, even arguing that slavery was an important biblical principle for proper civil organization. The master-slave relationship that Paul outlined was often interpreted to mean that slaves should see their masters as the temporal manifestation of God on earth and relate to those earthly masters as such. For further discussions on this subject, see Greene, *Negro in Colonial New England*, 285–87; Berlin, *Generations of Captivity*, 206–7; Ashworth, *Slavery, Capitalism, and Politics*, 210–12.

7. See Ashworth, *Slavery, Capitalism, and Politics*, 212–13.

8. In Ephesians 6:5, Paul writes, "Servants, be obedient to them that are your masters according to the flesh, with fear and trembling, in singleness of your heart, as unto Christ."

9. See Barck, *Papers of the Lloyd Family*, 109, 234, 307, 501. These passages and numerous others throughout the two-volume record of the Lloyd family manor point to the various ways that the Lloyds sold or otherwise "disposed" of their slaves.

10. Loggins, "Critical Analysis," states that Hammon's masters "undoubtedly allowed him to go freely to church, where he absorbed the doctrines of the Calvinist Methodists, of which all his work is an echo" (36). Hammon may have attended a Methodist church, but this is not certain, and the theology that serves as a foundation for his work appears to contradict Loggins's conclusion. While Hammon was certainly a Calvinist, his writing has more in common with the beliefs of Anglicans (the Episcopal Church) than of Methodists, who would have been viewed as a Dissenting sect of the church and whose views would have been less than welcome to an aristocratic family that such as the Lloyds, who still held strong allegiances to England and who helped to found an Episcopal church in nearby Huntington. Loggins, like many other scholars, labels Hammon a Calvinist, a Methodist, or a Protestant but does not examine what those designations mean in relation to the religious contexts of the period. Rather, readers are left with

a vague notion of Hammon as a religious man without any basis for what he and his contemporaries would have perceived as religiosity.

11. Hammon, *America's First Negro Poet,* 67, 68.

12. Ibid., 70.

13. See Gibson, *Two Letters,* 16–18. In fact, the lord bishop's rationale uses more secular logic than Scripture to support his method of teaching Christianity to slave children rather than to the resistant adults. Hammon's essay is a religious elaboration on the lord bishop's pragmatic solution to missionary efforts.

14. Ibid.

15. Hammon, *America's First Negro Poet,* 69–70.

16. Ibid., 70.

17. Ibid., 70–71.

18. Ibid.

19. Ibid., 75.

20. Ibid.

21. Ibid.

22. Barck, *Papers of the Lloyd Family,* 109–10, 113, 115, 261. These are just a small sample of the references to slaves in this sense.

23. Ibid., 704.

24. Ibid., 187.

25. See Berlin, *Generations of Captivity,* 281–82, 352–53; Foner, *Blacks in the American Revolution*; Nash, *Race and Revolution,* 171–76, 85–89.

26. See Hammon, *America's First Negro Poet,* 73–74.

27. See Moss, *Slavery on Long Island,* 182–83.

28. Ibid., 148. In *America's First Negro Poet,* Ransom mistakenly gives the title of this essay as "An Address to the Negroes of the State of New York." Hammon originally sent the essay as part of a September 24, 1786, letter to the members of the African Society of New York City.

29. Ibid., 148–49.

30. See Hammon, *America's First Negro Poet,* 112.

31. Ibid., 73.

32. See Hammon, "Address," 107–8.

33. See Hammon, *America's First Negro Poet,* 75, 77–78.

34. Ibid., 74.

35. Callahan, "Paul's Epistle to Philemon," 363–65.

36. Ibid., 362–63.

37. See Elwell, *Baker Theological Dictionary,* 740–41; see the entry on "Slavery" for further scholarly commentary on ancient laws concerning slavery and Paul's attitudes toward the subject.

38. Martin, *Ephesians, Colossians, and Philemon,* 73.

39. See Crossan, *Birth of Christianity,* 183–84.

40. See MacArthur, *MacArthur New Testament Commentary,* 324.

41. Murphy-O'Connor, *Paul,* 249.

42. See Davis, "Problem of Slavery," 20.

43. For a thorough explanation of how antislavery sentiment became a part of Christian moral thinking in the seventeenth and eighteenth centuries, see ibid., 20–25.

44. Christian tradition recognizes three phases of biblical history, the time before the messiah, the life and death of the messiah, and the return of the messiah after the resurrection. Hammon would have recognized that he lived in an intermediary period between the second and third ages of Christian history, waiting for the messiah's return.

45. See Hammon, *America's First Negro Poet*, 55, lines 19–20.

46. Ibid., lines 9–12.

47. Ibid., lines 33–36

48. Ibid., 56, lines 53–56.

49. Ibid., 108.

50. Philemon 1:1–25.

51. Ibid., 1:16.

52. See Peters, "Jupiter Hammon," 1, 6–9.

53. Hammon, *America's First Negro Poet*, 64, lines 61–68.

54. Ibid., 112.

55. Ibid., 112–13.

56. Ibid., 108.

57. In particular here, I am thinking about O'Neale, Stanley A. Ransom Jr., Peters, Loggins, and Richards. Each has done their own interesting and useful interpretation of Hammon's work and his significance as a black writer. Though Ransom and Loggins tend to dismiss Hammon's aesthetic sensibilities, O'Neale, Peters, and Richards take a more informed approach to Hammon's use of language, showing not only his sophisticated knowledge and use of Christian rhetorical tropes but also helping readers place Hammon's dialect within a continuum of African American language practices.

58. Hammon, *America's First Negro Poet*, 46, lines 63–68.

59. Ibid., 46, line 45, 45, lines 1, 4.

60. Ibid., 91.

61. Ibid., 88.

62. Ibid.

63. Ibid., 108.

64. Ibid., 110.

65. Ibid., 112.

66. Ibid.

67. Ibid., 31.

68. The question of whether slave spirituals were imitations of the European tradition of song or their own original innovation is an old one that has been answered quite well by scholars of music and history, who point out that like Christian worship, the black spiritual is an innovation that combined European and African traditions to create a unique musical form that very often entertained and even amazed white listeners with its aesthetic beauty. See Levine, "Slave Song and Slave Consciousness." See also White, *American Negro Folk-Songs*, 29, 55.

69. See Raboteau, *Slave Religion*, 67–74.

70. Hammon, *America's First Negro Poet*, 45, lines 1–4.

71. Ibid., 46, lines 63–68.

72. Raboteau, *Slave Religion*, 74.

Two. *Phillis Wheatley and the Charge toward Progressive Black Theologies*

1. Robinson, *Phillis Wheatley: A Bio-Bibliography*, 18–19.

2. Ibid., 1.

3. See, for example, Levernier, "Phillis Wheatley and the New England Clergy"; Isani, "Methodist Connection"; Shields, "Phillis Wheatley's Struggle."

4. See Smith, "Phillis Wheatley," 403; Jamison, "Analysis," 409. Although these evaluations come out of the same journal, such commentary was far from unusual during this period, as Richmond's more sympathetic, nevertheless negative, evaluation of her poetry suggests in *Bid the Vassal Soar*.

5. O'Neale, "Slave's Subtle Civil War," 144.

6. While Black Arts movement thinkers understandably attempted to define a "black aesthetic" by which to evaluate literature, as Bassard explains, "the tendency to equate vernacularity with authenticity" threatened to "dismiss much of the early black writers' work as somehow 'inauthentic' " (*Spiritual Interrogations*, 17). The linguistic and textual markers of authenticity were defined very narrowly in the case of interpretation. This superficially structuralist mode of analysis excluded many important early texts by black writers because only one acceptable and socially specific mode of expression was "authentic." "Thus the search for only externally recognizable textual signs fails adequately to contextualize the relations of power inhering in cultural forms of resistance" (18). There is, therefore, no single black vernacular, as some scholars came to propound, but a multiplicity of textual vernaculars adapted to the particular circumstances of social and cultural expression and resistance. The failure to recognize and theorize a multiplicity of African American vernaculars ultimately contributed to the larger cultural and political failures of the Black Arts and Black Power movements. In his essay, "Black Particularity Reconsidered," Reed explains that this aesthetic impulse of the nationalist wing of the Black Power movement "mistook artifacts and idiosyncrasies of culture for its totality and froze them into an ahistorical theory of authenticity" that caused black culture, in some senses, to lose its dynamism and take on the commodity form (52).

7. O'Neale, "Slave's Subtle Civil War," 147.

8. Jefferson, *Portable Thomas Jefferson*, 189.

9. Gates, "Phillis Wheatley on Trial," 38–39.

10. Robinson, *Critical Essays*, 22, 33–36.

11. Over the past two decades, a number of scholars, including Bassard, Dickson D. Bruce Jr., O'Neale, and Scheick, have provided nuanced examinations of Wheatley's writings.

12. Bassard, *Spiritual Interrogations*, 17–18.

13. Shields writes about Wheatley's epyllia in, "Phillis Wheatley's Use of Classicism."

14. Wheatley, *Collected Works*, 43, line 2.

15. Ibid., 43–44, lines 13–18.

16. Ibid., 44, lines 31–34.

17. Ibid., 45, lines 43–44.

18. Ibid., 15, lines 7–9.

19. Ibid., lines 10–12.

20. The term *Gospel* is an English rendering of the Greek *evangelon* and the Latin *evangelium*, meaning "good news." Wheatley's rendering of *Gospel* as "blissful news" attests to her knowledge of the word's etymology.

21. Sir Isaac Newton, for example, wrote in *Optics* (1704), "Whence is it that nature does nothing in vain, and whence arises all that order and beauty which we see in the world? To what end are comets, and whence is it that planets move all one and the same way in orbs concentric while comets move all manner of ways in orbs very eccentric, and what hinders the fixed stars from falling upon one another? . . . [D]oes it not appear from phenomena that there is a Being, incorporeal, living, intelligent, omnipresent, who in infinite space, as it were his sensory, sees the things themselves intimately and thoroughly perceives them, and comprehends them wholly by their immediate presence to himself?" Newton's characterization sounds remarkably similar to Wheatley's more poetic version of God's role as first mover. In a 1692 letter, Newton states even more bluntly, "The Motions which the Planets now have could not spring from any natural Cause alone, but were impressed by an intelligent Agent" (Kramnick, *Portable Enlightenment Reader*, 97–98). Further information about the beliefs of Enlightenment scientists and philosophers concerning God and religion appear in Bush, "Rational Proof."

22. Almost all of Wheatley's poems have a religious tone or use religious language. By "evangelical poem" in particular, however, I mean a poem written specifically for the purpose of proselytizing. "To the University of Cambridge in New England," "Goliath of Gath," "Thoughts on the Works of Providence," and "An Hymn to Humanity: To S.P.G. Esq." constitute the four evangelical poems in *Poems on Various Subjects*.

23. An excellent discussion of the apparent ambiguity of this combination of the classical tradition with eighteenth-century Christianity appears in Scheick, *Authority and Female Authorship*, 107–9. Scheick argues that part of Wheatley's aesthetic was the use of ambiguity to mask, to a degree, the political implications of her work. This ambiguity allowed her to engage in an "underground renunciation of slavery" that is evidenced through the "logonomic conflict," which, he argues, "gives the impression of a conscious choice" in her criticism of slavery (109–10).

24. For example, Jonathan Edwards was interested and influenced by the sciences. See Hornberger, "Effect of the New Science." Few religious thinkers of the time saw any contradiction between the use of and references to classical mythology in their writing: Because "the [classical] gods were so obviously not divine, so thoroughly identified with the natural world," these theologians felt "no particular aversion to the classical deities, who often appear in poems on the natural world" (Daly, *God's Altar*, 142–43).

25. Wheatley, *Collected Works*, vi. Although he makes some questionable claims about Wheatley's "demure" personality, see also Gates, *Trials of Phillis Wheatley*.

26. Wheatley, *Collected Works*, 159–60.

27. For a thorough examination of the extent and significance of Wheatley's revisions, see Bassard, *Spiritual Interrogations*, chapter 2.

28. "Letter to the Reverend Samson Occom," in Wheatley, *Collected Works*, 176–77.

29. Edwards similarly locates virtue within the individual human "heart," and that virtue is grounded in a love of God and his creations, leading toward virtuous actions with regard to both God and his creation. See Edwards, *Two Dissertations*.

30. Elwell, *Baker Theological Dictionary*, 375–76.

31. Wheatley, *Collected Works*, 61, lines 27–30.

32. Ibid., 17, lines 5–8.

33. A significantly different draft version of this poem, like many of those included in the 1773 collection, exists and is available in ibid., 202–3. That version of the poem has a very different tone and is less consistently pro–colonial American as the published version. I believe the differences between the two versions to be a product of changes in Wheatley's views regarding the revolutionary movement between 1768 and 1773.

34. Ibid., 82, lines 1–2.

35. Ibid., lines 5–6.

36. Ibid., 83, lines 15–18.

37. Ibid., lines 23–26.

38. Wheatley, *Collected Works*, 176.

39. Akers, " 'Our Modern Egyptians.' "

40. Bassard, *Spiritual Interrogations*, 45–46.

41. Pemberton and Wheatley, *Heaven the Residence of Saints*.

42. Hammon, *America's First Negro Poet*, 52, lines 65–68. See Eleanor Smith, "Phillis Wheatley"; Jamison, "Analysis"; Collins, "Phillis Wheatley."

43. Ibid., 52, lines 73–76.

44. See Wheatley, *Complete Writings*, 185.

45. Wheatley, *Collected Works*, 146, lines 39–42.

46. Wheatley, *Complete Writings*, 100.

47. See Akers, "Religion and the American Revolution," 497.

48. Wheatley, *Complete Writings*, 102–3.

Three. *John Marrant and the Narrative Construction of an Early Black Methodist Evangelical*

1. Blakeley and Grant, *Eleven Exiles*, 13. See also James Walker, *Black Loyalists*.

2. Brooks, "Journal of John Marrant," 15.

3. Gustafson, *Eloquence Is Power*, 107–8.

4. Hodges, *Root and Branch*, 140–60, discusses the apparent paradox of black loyalists and black revolutionaries fighting toward the same goals.

5. Gustafson, *Eloquence Is Power*, 101.

6. Edwards, *Great Awakening*, 7.

7. For a thorough treatment of the background for Marrant's theology, see Saillant, " 'Wipe Away All Tears from Their Eyes.' "

8. See Carretta, *Unchained Voices*, 131, see also 131 n.55. For more on Spa Fields Chapel, see Schlenther, *Queen of the Methodists*.

9. Schlenther, *Queen of the Methodists*, 145.

10. Ibid., 152.

11. Marrant, "Narrative," 126.

12. Ibid., 125–26.

13. See Equiano, *Interesting Narrative*. The narrative includes numerous examples of Equiano contending with the impieties of his fellow sailors.

14. See Whitchurch, *Negro Convert*, lines 252–60.

15. Schlenther, *Queen of the Methodists*, 2.

16. Marrant, "Narrative," 126.

17. Benilde Montgomery discusses how Marrant's *Narrative* fell out of literary and historical studies after its 1835 edition in "Recapturing John Marrant," in Shuffelton, *Mixed Race*, 105–6. Montgomery argues that because Marrant identifies himself as "black" only twice in the *Narrative*, abolitionists and Protestant nativists were not interested in his work.

18. Marrant, "Narrative," 126–27.

19. See Wood, " 'Jesus Christ Has got Thee at Last,' " 5.

20. Marrant, "Narrative," 128.

21. Ibid., 127.

22. Saillant, " 'Wipe all Tears from Their Eyes,' " 6.

23. Ibid., 6–7.

24. Marrant, "Narrative," 124.

25. Ibid.

26. Gibson, *Two Letters*, 8, 18.

27. Ibid., 24.

28. Ibid., 16.

29. Marrant, "Narrative," 124.

30. Ibid.

31. Schlenther, *Queen of the Methodists*, 90–91.

32. Ibid., 91.

33. Marrant, "Narrative," 129. Carretta has uncovered records that indicate that a John Marrant of Charleston owned three slaves. The relationship of these documents to the John Marrant under discussion here is not yet fully known. He may have bought the three out of slavery, as was the case many times in which family members bought one another to save them from the institution. Marrant may never have advocated antislavery, which would have been consistent with the beliefs of his benefactor, the Countess of Huntingdon; however, such a position would contradict the message of his ministry in Nova Scotia and Boston. The owner of the slaves could also be a completely different man with the same name.

34. Schlenther, *Queen of the Methodists*, 90–91.

35. Ibid., 91.

36. Marrant, "Narrative," 123.

37. In addition to Raboteau, *Slave Religion*, 212–19, see Aptheker, *American Negro Slave*

Revolts; Raboteau, *African American Religion*; Woodson, *History of the Negro Church*, 2nd ed. All of these foundational histories address in greater detail the early structure and development of African American religious practices.

38. Marrant, "Narrative," 123.

39. Woodson, *History of the Negro Church*, 2nd ed., 50–51.

40. Horton and Edwards, *Backgrounds in American Literary Thought*, 29–48.

41. Schlenther, *Queen of the Methodists*, 146.

42. See Macroberts, "Black Roots of Pentecostalism," 192.

43. Marrant, "Narrative," 111.

44. Raboteau, *Slave Religion*, 132–50.

45. Marrant, *Sermon*, 126–27.

46. See Andrews, *To Tell a Free Story*, 18–19.

47. Marrant, *Journal*, A2.

48. Ibid., v.

49. Ibid.

50. Ibid., 4.

51. Ibid., A2.

52. Schlenther, *Queen of the Methodists*, 163.

53. Marrant, *Journal*, 44.

Four. *Prince Hall and the Influence of Revolutionary Enlightenment Philosophy on the Institutionalization of Black Religion*

1. See Hall, "Pray God," 49.

2. Not long after Hall became free, he signed a petition to end slavery in Massachusetts. See Kaplan, *Black Presence*, 202.

3. See Immanuel Kant, "What Is the Enlightenment?" in Kramnick, *Portable Enlightenment Reader*, 1.

4. Ibid.

5. Paine, *Rights of Man*, 210.

6. Hall, "Pray God," 49.

7. For further information on Hall's life and social context, see Grimshaw, *Official History*. However, Grimshaw's early study should be supplemented by more contemporary scholarship that cuts through much of the apocrypha, such as Bullock, *Revolutionary Brotherhood*; Gray, *Inside Prince Hall*; Walkes, *Black Square and Compass*; Wesley, *Prince Hall*.

8. Hall, "Pray God," 51–52.

9. Hodges, *Root and Branch*, 183–84.

10. Andrews, *To Tell a Free Story*, 5.

11. Ibid., 6.

12. Ibid., 36–37.

13. See Douglass, *My Bondage and My Freedom*, 361–62.

14. Marrant, "You Stand," 29.

15. Newman, Rael, and Lapsansky, *Pamphlets of Protest*, 8.

16. Brooks, *American Lazarus*, 121–23.

17. Thornton, *Africa and Africans, 1400–1800*, 304.

18. Davis, "Constitution and the Slave Trade," 22.

19. Ibid., 23.

20. Hall, "Charge Delivered," 40.

21. Ibid.

22. Davis and Mintz, *Boisterous Sea of Liberty*, 226–27.

23. Marrant, "You Stand," 32.

24. Hall, "Charge Delivered," 40–41.

25. Paine, *Rights of Man*, 411–15.

26. Ibid., 425.

27. Thornton, *Africa and Africans, 1400–1800*, 296.

28. Ibid., 293.

29. Aptheker, *American Negro Slave Revolts*, 18.

30. Thornton, *Africa and Africans, 1400–1800*, 317.

31. Aptheker, *American Negro Slave Revolts*, 68.

32. Ibid., 67–70.

33. Hall, "Charge Delivered," 43.

34. Ibid., 46.

35. Ibid., 48.

36. David Walker, *David Walker's Appeal*, xii.

37. See Easton, "Treatise," 106–7.

38. See Lapsansky, " 'Since They Got Those Separate Churches.' "

39. Hall, "Pray God," 48–49.

40. Ibid., 49.

41. Ibid.

42. Ibid., 52.

Five. *Richard Allen and the Further Institutionalization of Black Theologies*

1. Allen, Life, Experience, and Gospel Labours, 13.

2. Raboteau, *Fire in the Bones*, 80.

3. Cannon, *Theology of John Wesley*, 15.

4. Nash, "New Light on Richard Allen," 337.

5. Allen, *Life, Experience, and Gospel Labours*, 12.

6. Ibid.

7. Ibid., 13–14.

8. Ibid., 14.

9. Woodson, *History of the Negro Church*, 2nd ed., 61.

10. Rush, *Letters*, 599–600.

11. Ibid., 600.

12. Ibid., 608.

13. Allen, *Life, Experience, and Gospel Labours*, 16.

14. Raboteau, *Fire in the Bones*, 87–88.

15. Allen, *Life, Experience, and Gospel Labours*, 16.

16. Absalom Jones, "Petition of Absalom Jones and Seventy-three Others," in Porter, *Early Negro Writing*, 330.

17. Ibid., 331.

18. Nash, "New Light on Richard Allen," 335. At this time, there is no definite record of the date when Allen's mother and siblings were sold, but Nash speculates that it was probably 1776, and I agree as the dates coincide with the time in Allen's life in which he "awakens" to discover himself "wrenched and undone."

19. Allen, *Life, Experience, and Gospel Labours*, 5.

20. Eagleton, *Idea of Culture*, 1.

21. Ibid., 4.

22. Allen, *Life, Experience, and Gospel Labours*, 12.

23. Elwell, *Baker Theological Dictionary*, 143–44 (entry on "David").

24. David Walker, *David Walker's Appeal*, 60–61.

25. Allen, *Doctrines and Discipline*, 9, 39.

26. Allen, *Life, Experience, and Gospel Labours*, 3.

27. Ibid., 5.

28. Ibid.

29. Ibid., 7.

30. Ibid., 6.

31. Ibid., 7.

32. Ibid., 10.

33. Allen, *Life, Experience, and Gospel Labours*, 12.

34. Rush, *Letters*, 608, 1070.

35. David Walker, *David Walker's Appeal*, 4.

36. Rush, *Letters*, 624.

37. Ibid., 636, 639.

38. The most thorough discussion of the yellow fever epidemic in Philadelphia and Allen's activities during the crisis appears in Brooks, *American Lazarus*, 151–81.

39. Jones and Allen, *Narrative*, 33.

40. Rush, *Letters*, 654.

41. Ibid., 684.

42. Ibid., 731.

43. Allen, *Life, Experience, and Gospel Labours*, 44.

44. Raboteau, *Fire in the Bones*, 87.

45. Magaw, *Discourse*, 76.

46. Ibid.

47. Ibid., 77.

48. Ibid.

49. Ibid., 78.

50. Ibid., 80.

51. Ibid., 80–81.
52. Ibid., 81.
53. Ibid.
54. Woodson, *History of the Negro Church*, 2nd ed., 81.
55. Jones and Allen, *Narrative*, 42.
56. Ibid.
57. Jones, *Causes and Motives*, 94.
58. Ibid.
59. Ibid., 95.
60. Allen, *Life, Experience, and Gospel Labours*, 15.
61. Raboteau, *Fire in the Bones*, 87.
62. Allen, *Life, Experience, and Gospel Labours*, 18.
63. Raboteau, *Fire in the Bones*, 91.
64. Ibid.
65. Allen, *Life, Experience, and Gospel Labours*, 21.

Six. *Maria Stewart and the Mission of Black Women in Evangelicalism*

1. This tendency to define universality in masculine terms makes the cultural representation of black female subjectivity particularly difficult. Historically, as Connor has pointed out in *Conversions and Visions*, 74–75, black women writers who were educated and could not be easily exoticized, such as E. W. Harper and Maria Stewart, remained virtually unknown beyond a limited milieu. Other black women speakers and writers, such as Sojourner Truth, described by Harriet Beecher Stowe as the "Libyan Sibil," enjoyed much more visibility and fame among abolitionist circles, as commentators could reduce the individual personae of these women to the status of the exotic primitive. Wheatley avoided this obscurity, in her own day and subsequently for a substantial time by historians, even though she was unusually educated for an African American slave. Alternately exoticized as a consequence of her personal origin and circumstance as an African and slave and exceptional because of her facility with the English language, Wheatley existed in an ambiguous middle ground between racialized identities and institutions of power, and her writing, though in many ways universalizing, liberatory, and resistant, tended to be couched in masculine terms that gave her greater cachet as she navigated the fields of language and power in which she operated. Other black women writers, though every bit as educated and articulate, tended to write in a different context. Usually they were free, American-born individuals who not only questioned slavery and racial oppression but also challenged gender conventions, and black and white audiences chastised or ignored these women for their efforts. See also Bassard, *Spiritual Interrogations*, 76.
2. Stewart, "Religion," 28–29.
3. Ibid.
4. Peterson has argued that this complex use of biblical rhetoric, infused with "Africanisms and African Americanisms," served as a means of testing and overcoming the "prohibitions placed on black women by the power structures of black male institu-

tions" (*Doers of the Word,* 56–57). Stewart found these institutions lacking because of their exclusion of women as active leaders. Indeed Stewart not only quotes Scripture in her critiques but becomes a living embodiment of the archetypal Old Testament prophet commissioned by God to speak directly to black communities and state the requirements for achieving relief from worldly oppressions. Stewart argues, just as Jeremiah contended for the Hebrews, that these oppressions signify God's discontent with the individual and collective conduct of the nation or of his chosen people. As Peterson has noted, this turn in black textual production represents a reconfiguration of the genres of spiritual writing within the Western literary tradition.

5. Edwards describes early conversion experiences in *A Faithful Narrative of the Surprising Work of God,* in *Works of Jonathan Edwards,* 344–64.

6. Stewart, "Religion," 29.

7. Ibid.

8. Ibid., 30.

9. In the first chapter of her excellent study on the spiritual narratives of nineteenth-century African American women, Moody has noted that both Stewart's 1835 compilation of her works, *Productions of Maria W. Stewart,* and her 1879 revision of the same collection of works, *Meditations from the Pen of Mrs. Maria W. Stewart,* contain autobiographical elements that allow insight into her life. According to Moody, Stewart's complete works constitute a form of autobiography identified as the black jeremiad (*Sentimental Confessions,* 29). My study identifies the theological elements of Stewart's early writings before they are compiled rather than the autobiographical material that has already been identified in Moody's work.

10. Stewart, "Religion," 30.

11. Stewart, *Maria W. Stewart,* 52.

12. Stewart, "Religion," 31.

13. Amos 7:14–15.

14. Stewart, "Mrs. Stewart's Farewell Address," 68.

15. Ibid., 69.

16. Stewart's *Meditations,* therefore, constitute more than a simple collection of prayers or emotional outpourings that travel unidirectionally and passively to a remote divinity; rather, her work is a "discursive prayer" that "proceeds by discursive steps to build up a vision of things . . . aimed at arousing the will to acts of fervor" (Peterson, *Doers of the Word,* 59). The *Meditations* represent an active and activating form of communication with divinity that highlights the social aspect of Stewart's theology, making her more prone to petition for radical social change as part of God's mandate (61–62).

17. See Peterson's discussion of Stewart's identification with Old Testament Hebrew prophets (*Doers of the Word,* 62–63).

18. Stewart, "Religion," 33–34.

19. Isaiah 1:11, 13, 17.

20. Stewart, "Religion," 35.

21. Ibid., 32.

22. See Wheatley's letter to Samsom Occom in Wheatley, *Collected Works,* 177.

23. Bercovitch, *American Jeremiad*, 34–35.

24. Felder, *Troubling Biblical Waters*, 61.

25. Ibid., 63.

26. Stewart, "Religion," 35.

27. Ibid., 37.

28. Ibid.

29. Ibid.

30. Stewart, "Mrs. Stewart's Farewell Address," 68.

31. Ibid.

BIBLIOGRAPHY

Akers, Charles W. " 'Our Modern Egyptians': Phillis Wheatley and the Whig Campaign against Slavery in Revolutionary Boston." *Journal of Negro History* 60, no. 3 (1975): 397–410.

———. "Religion and the American Revolution: Samuel Cooper and the Brattle Street Church." *William and Mary Quarterly*, 3rd ser., 35, no. 3 (1978): 447–49.

Allen, Richard. *The Doctrines and Discipline of the African Methodist Episcopal Church.* Philadelphia: Allen and Tapisco for the African Methodist Connection in the United States, 1817.

———. *The Life, Experience, and Gospel Labours of the Rt. Rev. Richard Allen: To Which Is Annexed the Rise and Progress of the African Methodist Episcopal Church in the United States of America; Containing a Narrative of the Yellow Fever in the Year of Our Lord 1793; with an Address to the People of Colour in the United States; Written by Himself, and Published by His Request.* Philadelphia: Martin and Boden, 1833.

Andrews, William L. *To Tell a Free Story: The First Century of Afro-American Autobiography, 1760–1865.* Urbana: University of Illinois Press, 1986.

Aptheker, Herbert. *American Negro Slave Revolts.* New ed. New York: International, 1969.

———. *Negro Slave Revolts in the United States, 1526–1860.* New York: International, 1939.

Ashworth, John. *Slavery, Capitalism, and Politics in the Antebellum Republic.* Vol. 1, *Commerce and Compromise, 1820–1850.* New York: Cambridge University Press, 1995.

Barck, Dorothy C., ed. *Papers of the Lloyd Family of the Manor of Queens Village, Lloyd's Neck, Long Island, New York, 1654–1826.* New York: New-York Historical Society, 1927.

Bassard, Katherine Clay. *Spiritual Interrogations: Culture, Gender, and Community in Early African American Women's Writing.* Princeton: Princeton University Press, 1999.

Bercovitch, Sacvan. *The American Jeremiad.* Madison: University of Wisconsin Press, 1978.

Berlin, Ira. "From Creole to African: Atlantic Creoles and the Origins of African-American Society in Mainland North America." In *How Did American Slavery Begin?* edited by Edward Countryman, 17–63. Boston: Bedford/St. Martin's, 1999.

———. *Generations of Captivity: A History of African-American Slaves.* Cambridge: Belknap Press of Harvard University Press, 2003.

Blakeley, Phyllis R., and John N. Grant. *Eleven Exiles: Accounts of Loyalists of the American Revolution.* Toronto: Dundurn, 1982.

Bourne, George. *The Book and Slavery Irreconcilable: With Animadversions upon Dr. Smith's Philosophy.* Philadelphia: Sanderson, 1816.

Brooks, Joanna. *American Lazarus: Religion and the Rise of African-American and Native American Literatures.* New York: Oxford University Press, 2003.

———. "The Journal of John Marrant: Providence and Prophecy in the Eighteenth-Century Black Atlantic." *North Star: A Journal of African American Religious History* 3, no. 1 (1999). http://northstar.vassar.edu.

Bullock, Steven C. *Revolutionary Brotherhood: Freemasonry and the Transformation of the American Social Order, 1730–1840.* Chapel Hill: University of North Carolina Press, 1996.

Bush, May Dulaney. "Rational Proof of a Deity from the Order of Nature." *ELH* 9, no. 4 (1942): 288–319.

Callahan, Allen Dwight. "Paul's Epistle to Philemon: Toward an Alternative Argumentum." *Harvard Theological Review* 86, no. 4 (1993): 357–76.

Cannon, William Ragsdale. *The Theology of John Wesley, with Special Reference to the Doctrine of Justification.* New York: Abingdon, 1946.

Carretta, Vincent, ed. *Unchained Voices: An Anthology of Black Authors in the English-Speaking World of the Eighteenth Century.* Lexington: University Press of Kentucky, 1996.

Close, Stacey K. *Elderly Slaves of the Plantation South.* New York: Garland, 1997.

Collins, Terence. "Phillis Wheatley: The Dark Side of the Poetry." *Phylon* 36, no. 1 (1975): 78–88.

Connor, Kimberly Rae. *Conversions and Visions in the Writings of African-American Women.* Knoxville: University of Tennessee Press, 1994.

Creel, Margaret Washington. *A Peculiar People: Slave Religion and Community-Culture among the Gullahs.* New York: New York University Press, 1988.

Crossan, John Dominic. *The Birth of Christianity: Discovering What Happened in the Years Immediately after the Execution of Jesus.* New York: HarperCollins, 1998.

Daly, Robert. *God's Altar: The World and the Flesh in Puritan Poetry.* Berkeley: University of California Press, 1978.

Darsey, James Francis. *The Prophetic Tradition and Radical Rhetoric in America.* New York: New York University Press, 1997.

Davis, David Brion. "The Constitution and the Slave Trade." In *American Negro Slavery: A Modern Reader*, 3rd ed., edited by Allen Weinstein, Frank Otto Gatell, and David Sarasohn, 21–32. New York: Oxford University Press, 1979.

———. "The Problem of Slavery in the Age of Revolution, 1770–1823." In *The Antislavery Debate: Capitalism and Abolitionism as a Problem in Historical Interpretation*, edited by Thomas Bender, 15–103. Berkeley: University of California Press, 1992.

Davis, David Brion, and Steven Mintz. *The Boisterous Sea of Liberty: A Documentary History of America from Discovery through the Civil War.* New York: Oxford University Press, 1998.

D'Elia, Donald J. "Dr. Benjamin Rush and the Negro." *Journal of the History of Ideas* 30, no. 3 (1969): 413–22.

Douglass, Frederick. *My Bondage and My Freedom.* New York: Dover, 1969.

Du Bois, W. E. B., ed. *The Negro Church: Report of a Social Study Made under the Direction of Atlanta University; Together with the Proceedings of the Eighth Conference for the Study of the Negro Problems, Held at Atlanta University, May 26th, 1903.* Atlanta: Atlanta University Press, 1903.

———. *The Souls of Black Folk.* Chicago: McClurg, 1903.

Eagleton, Terry. *The Idea of Culture.* Malden, Mass.: Blackwell, 2000.

Easton, Hosea. "A Treatise on the Intellectual Character, and the Civil and Political Condition of the Colored People of the United States." In *To Heal the Scourge of Prejudice: The Life and Writings of Hosea Easton,* edited by George R. Price and James Brewer Stewart, 63–121. Amherst: University of Massachusetts Press, 1999.

Edwards, Jonathan. *The Great Awakening: A Faithful Narrative.* Edited by C. C. Goen. New Haven: Yale University Press, 1972.

———. *Two Dissertations: I. Concerning the End for Which God Created the World; II. The Nature of True Virtue.* Boston: Kneeland, 1765.

———. *The Works of Jonathan Edwards.* Edited by Sereno Edwards Dwight and Edward Hickman. Edinburgh: Banner of Truth Trust, 1974.

Elwell, Walter A. *Baker Theological Dictionary of the Bible.* Grand Rapids, Mich.: Baker, 2000.

Equiano, Olaudah. *The Interesting Narrative and Other Writings.* Edited by Vincent Carretta. New York: Penguin, 1995.

Felder, Cain Hope. *Troubling Biblical Waters: Race, Class, and Family.* Maryknoll, N.Y.: Orbis, 1989.

Foner, Philip S. *Blacks in the American Revolution.* Westport, Conn.: Greenwood, 1976.

Foner, Philip S., and Robert J. Branham. *Lift Every Voice: African American Oratory, 1787–1900.* Tuscaloosa: University of Alabama Press, 1998.

Frey, Sylvia R. *Water from the Rock: Black Resistance in a Revolutionary Age.* Princeton: Princeton University Press, 1991.

Frey, Sylvia R., and Betty Wood. *Come Shouting to Zion: African American Protestantism in the American South and British Caribbean to 1830.* Chapel Hill: University of North Carolina Press, 1998.

Garrison, William Lloyd. *The Letters of William Lloyd Garrison.* Edited by Walter McIntosh Merrill and Louis Ruchames. Cambridge: Belknap Press of Harvard University Press, 1971.

Gates, Henry Louis, Jr. "Phillis Wheatley on Trial: In 1772, a Slave Girl Had to Prove She Was a Poet; She's Had to Do So Ever Since." *New Yorker,* January 20, 2003, 82–87.

———. *The Trials of Phillis Wheatley.* New York: BasicCivitas, 2003.

George, Carol V. R. *Segregated Sabbaths: Richard Allen and the Emergence of Independent Black Churches, 1760–1840.* New York: Oxford University Press, 1973.

Gibson, Edmund. *Observations upon the Conduct and Behaviour of a Certain Sect, Usually Distinguished by the Name of Methodists.* N.p., 1740.

———. *Two Letters of the Lord Bishop of London, to Encourage and Promote the Instruction of Their Negroes in the Christian Faith.* London: Downing, 1727.

Gould, Philip. *Barbaric Traffic: Commerce and Antislavery in the Eighteenth-Century Atlantic World.* Cambridge: Harvard University Press, 2003.

Gray, David L. *Inside Prince Hall.* Lancaster, Va.: Lancaster Communications, 2003.

Greene, Lorenzo Johnston. *The Negro in Colonial New England, 1620–1776.* Port Washington, N.Y.: Kennikat, 1966.

Grimshaw, William H. *Official History of Freemasonry among the Colored People in North America: Tracing the Growth of Masonry from 1717 down to the Present Day.* New York: Broadway, 1903.

Guruswamy, Rosemary Fithian. " 'Thou Hast the Holy Word': Jupiter Hammon's 'Regards' to Phillis Wheatley." In *Genius in Bondage: Literature of the Early Black Atlantic,* edited by Vincent Carretta, 190–98. Lexington: University Press of Kentucky, 2001.

Gustafson, Sandra M. *Eloquence Is Power: Oratory and Performance in Early America.* Chapel Hill: University of North Carolina Press, 2000.

Hall, Prince. "A Charge Delivered to the Brethren of the African Lodge." In *Lift Every Voice: African American Oratory, 1787–1900,* edited by Philip S. Foner and Robert J. Branham, 38–45. Tuscaloosa: University of Alabama Press, 1998.

————. "Pray God Give Us the Strength to Bear Up under All Our Troubles." In *Lift Every Voice: African American Oratory, 1787–1900,* edited by Philip S. Foner and Robert J. Branham, 45–52. Tuscaloosa: University of Alabama Press, 1998.

Hammon, Jupiter. "An Address to the Negroes of the State of New York." In *America's First Negro Poet: The Complete Works of Jupiter Hammon of Long Island,* edited by Stanley Austin Ransom Jr., 103–18. Port Washington, N.Y.: Friedman Division, Kennikat, 1970.

————. *America's First Negro Poet: The Complete Works of Jupiter Hammon of Long Island.* Edited by Stanley Austin Ransom Jr. Port Washington, N.Y.: Friedman Division, Kennikat, 1970.

Hegel, Georg Wilhelm Friedrich. *The Philosophy of History.* New York: Dover, 1956.

Herskovits, Melville. *The Myth of the Negro Past.* Boston: Beacon, 1958.

Hodges, Graham Russell. *Root and Branch: African Americans in New York and East Jersey, 1613–1863.* Chapel Hill: University of North Carolina Press, 1999.

Hopkins, Samuel. *A Dialogue, Concerning the Slavery of the Africans; Shewing It to Be the Duty and Interest of the American Colonies to Emancipate All Their African Slaves: With an Address to the Owners of Such Slaves.* Norwich, Conn.: Spooner, 1776.

Hornberger, Theodore. "The Effect of the New Science upon the Thought of Jonathan Edwards." *American Literature* 9, no. 2 (1937): 196–207.

Horton, Rod William, and Herbert W. Edwards. *Backgrounds of American Literary Thought.* 2nd ed. New York: Appleton-Century-Crofts, 1967.

Isani, Mukhtar Ali. "The Methodist Connection: New Variants of Some Phillis Wheatley Poems." *Early American Literature* 22, no. 1 (1987): 108–13,

Jamison, Angelene. "Analysis of Selected Poetry of Phillis Wheatley." *Journal of Negro Education* 43, no. 3 (1974): 408–16.

Jefferson, Thomas. *The Portable Thomas Jefferson*. Edited by Merrill D. Peterson. New York: Penguin, 1977.

John, Beverly M. "The Construction of Racial Meaning by Blacks and Whites in Plantation Society." In *Plantation Society and Race Relations: The Origins of Inequality*, edited by Thomas J. Durant Jr. and J. Davis Knottnerus, 41–50. Westport, Conn.: Praeger, 1999.

Jones, Absalom. *The Causes and Motives for Establishing St. Thomas African Church of Philadelphia*. In *Annals of the First African Church, in the United States of America, Now Styled the African Episcopal Church of St. Thomas, Philadelphia*, edited by William Douglass, 93–95. Philadelphia: King and Baird, 1862.

Jones, Absalom, and Richard Allen. *A Narrative of the Proceedings of the Black People during the Late Awful Calamity in Philadelphia*. In *Pamphlets of Protest: An Anthology of Early African-American Protest Literature, 1790–1860*, edited by Richard Newman, Patrick Rael, and Phillip Lapsansky, 33–42. New York: Routledge, 2001.

Jordan, Winthrop D. *The White Man's Burden: Historical Origins of Racism in the United States*. New York: Oxford University Press, 1974.

————. *White over Black: American Attitudes toward the Negro, 1550–1812*. New York: Norton, 1977.

Kaplan, Sidney. *The Black Presence in the Era of the American Revolution, 1770–1800*. Greenwich, Conn.: New York Graphic Society, 1973.

Knox, Ronald Arbuthnott. *Enthusiasm: A Chapter in the History of Religion, with Special Reference to the XVII and XVIII Centuries*. New York: Oxford University Press, 1950.

Kramnick, Isaac, ed. *The Portable Enlightenment Reader*. New York: Penguin, 1995.

Lambert, Frank. *Inventing the "Great Awakening."* Princeton: Princeton University Press, 1999.

Lapsansky, Emma Jones. " 'Since They Got Those Separate Churches': Afro-Americans and Racism in Jacksonian Philadelphia." *American Quarterly* 32, no. 1 (1980): 54–78.

Levernier, James A. "Phillis Wheatley and the New England Clergy." *Early American Literature* 26, no. 1 (1991): 21–38.

Levine, Lawrence W. *Black Culture and Black Consciousness: Afro-American Folk Thought from Slavery to Freedom*. New York: Oxford University Press, 1977.

————. "Slave Song and Slave Consciousness." In *American Negro Slavery: A Modern Reader*, 3rd ed., edited by Allen Weinstein, Frank Otto Gatell, and David Sarasohn, 143–72. New York: Oxford University Press, 1979.

Loggins, Vernon. "Critical Analysis of the Works of Jupiter Hammon." In *America's First Negro Poet: The Complete Works of Jupiter Hammon of Long Island*, edited by Stanley Austin Ransom Jr., 35–41. Port Washington, N.Y.: Friedman Division, Kennikat, 1970.

Losonsky, Michael. *Enlightenment and Action from Descartes to Kant: Passionate Thought*. New York: Cambridge University Press, 2001.

MacArthur, John F. *The Macarthur New Testament Commentary: Ephesians*. Chicago: Moody Bible Institute, 1986.

Macroberts, Iain. "The Black Roots of Pentecostalism." In *Down by the Riverside: Readings in African American Religion,* edited by Larry G. Murphy, 189–99. New York: New York University Press, 2000.

Magaw, Samuel. *A Discourse Delivered July 17th, 1794, in the African Church of the City of Philadelphia, on the Occasion of Opening the Said Church, and Holding Public Worship in the First Time.* In *Annals of the First African Church, in the United States of America, Now Styled the African Episcopal Church of St. Thomas, Philadelphia,* edited by William Douglass, 58–83. Philadelphia: King and Baird, 1862.

Marrant, John. *A Journal of the Rev. John Marrant, from August the 18th, 1785, to the 16th of March, 1790.* London: Taylor and Marrant, 1790.

———. *A Narrative of the Lord's Wonderful Dealings with John Marrant, a Black.* In *Unchained Voices: An Anthology of Black Authors in the English-Speaking World of the Eighteenth Century,* edited by Vincent Carretta, 110–33. Lexington: University Press of Kentucky, 1996.

———. *A Sermon Preached on the 24th Day of June 1789, Being the Festival of St. John the Baptist, at the Request of the Right Worshipful the Grand Master Prince Hall, and the Rest of the Brethren of the African Lodge of the Honorable Society of Free and Accepted Masons in Boston.* Boston: Bible and Heart, 1789.

———. "You Stand on the Level with the Greatest Kings on Earth." In *Lift Every Voice: African American Oratory, 1787–1900,* ed. Philip S. Foner and Robert J. Branham, 27–38. Tuscaloosa: University of Alabama Press, 1998.

Martin, Ralph P. *Ephesians, Colossians, and Philemon.* Atlanta: Knox, 1991.

Mather, Cotton. *The Negro Christianized: An Essay to Excite and Assist the Good Work, the Instruction of Negro-Servants in Christianity.* Boston: Green, 1706.

Moody, Joycelyn. *Sentimental Confessions: Spiritual Narratives of Nineteenth-Century African American Women.* Athens: University of Georgia Press, 2001.

Morgan, Philip D. *Slave Counterpoint: Black Culture in the Eighteenth-Century Chesapeake and Lowcountry.* Chapel Hill: University of North Carolina Press, 1998.

Moss, Richard Shannon. *Slavery on Long Island: A Study in Local Institutional and Early African-American Communal Life.* New York: Garland, 1993.

Murphy-O'Connor, Jerome. *Paul: A Critical Life.* Oxford: Clarendon, 1996.

Nash, Gary B. "New Light on Richard Allen: The Early Years of Freedom." *William and Mary Quarterly,* 3rd ser., 46, no. 2 (1989): 332–40.

———. *Race and Revolution.* Madison, Wis.: Madison House, 1990.

Newman, Richard, Patrick Rael, and Phillip Lapsansky, eds. *Pamphlets of Protest: An Anthology of Early African-American Protest Literature, 1790–1860.* New York: Routledge, 2001.

Nietzsche, Friedrich Wilhelm. *The Birth of Tragedy out of the Spirit of Music.* Edited by Michael Tanner. New York: Penguin, 1993.

O'Neale, Sondra A. *Jupiter Hammon and the Biblical Beginnings of African-American Literature.* Metuchen, N.J.: Scarecrow, 1993.

———. "A Slave's Subtle Civil War: Phillis Wheatley's Use of Biblical Myth and Symbol." *Early American Literature* 21, no. 1 (1986): 144–65.

Paine, Thomas. *Rights of Man, Common Sense, and Other Political Writings.* Edited by Mark Philip. Oxford: Oxford University Press, 1995.

Patterson, Orlando. *Slavery and Social Death: A Comparative Study.* Cambridge: Harvard University Press, 1982.

Pemberton, Ebenezer, and Phillis Wheatley. *Heaven the Residence of Saints: A Sermon Occasioned by the Sudden and Much Lamented Death of the Rev. George Whitefield, A.M., Chaplain to the Right Honourable the Countess of Huntington.* Boston: Dilly, 1771.

Peters, Erskine. "Jupiter Hammon: His Engagement with Interpretation." *Journal of Ethnic Studies* 8, no. 4 (1981): 1–12.

Peterson, Carla L. *Doers of the Word: African-American Women Speakers and Writers in the North, 1830–1880.* New York: Oxford University Press, 1995.

Plato. *Phaedrus and the Seventh and Eighth Letters.* Translated by Walter Hamilton. Harmondsworth: Penguin, 1973.

———. *The Last Days of Socrates: The Apology, Crito, and Phaedo.* Translated by Hugh Tredennick. London: Penguin, 1954.

Porter, Dorothy, ed. *Early Negro Writing, 1760–1837.* Boston: Beacon, 1971.

Raboteau, Albert J. *African American Religion.* New York: Oxford University Press, 1999.

———. *A Fire in the Bones: Reflections on African-American Religious History.* Boston: Beacon, 1995.

———. *Slave Religion: The "Invisible Institution" in the Antebellum South.* New York: Oxford University Press, 1978.

Reed, Adolph L. "Black Particularity Reconsidered." In *Is It Nation Time? Contemporary Essays on Black Power and Black Nationalism,* edited by Eddie S. Glaude, 39–66. Chicago: University of Chicago Press, 2002.

Richards, Philip M. "Nationalist Themes in the Preaching of Jupiter Hammon." *Early American Literature* 25, no. 2 (1990): 123–31.

Richmond, M. A. *Bid the Vassal Soar: Interpretive Essays on the Life and Poetry of Phillis Wheatley and George Moses Horton.* Washington, D.C.: Howard University Press, 1974.

Robinson, William H., ed. *Critical Essays on Phillis Wheatley.* Boston: Hall, 1982.

———. *Phillis Wheatley: A Bio-Bibliography.* Boston: Hall, 1981.

———. "Phillis Wheatley in London." *College Language Association Journal* 21 (December 1977): 187–201.

Rush, Benjamin. *An Address on the Slavery of the Negroes in America.* New York: Arno, 1969.

———. *Letters.* Edited by L. H. Butterfield. Princeton: Princeton University Press for the American Philosophical Society, 1951.

Saillant, John. " 'Wipe Away All Tears from Their Eyes': John Marrant's Theology in the Black Atlantic, 1785–1808." *Journal of Millennial Studies* 1, no. 2 (1999). http://www.mille.org/publications/winter98/saillant.pdf.

Sandiford, Keith A. *Measuring the Moment: Strategies of Protest in Eighteenth-Century Afro-English Writing.* Cranbury, N.J.: Associated University Presses, 1988.

Scheick, William J. *Authority and Female Authorship in Colonial America*. Lexington: University Press of Kentucky, 1998.

Schlenther, Boyd Stanley. *Queen of the Methodists: The Countess of Huntingdon and the Eighteenth-Century Crisis of Faith and Society*. Durham, U.K.: Durham Academic, 1997.

Sensbach, Jon F. *A Separate Canaan: The Making of an Afro-Moravian World in North Carolina, 1763–1840*. Chapel Hill: University of North Carolina Press, 1998.

Sernett, Milton C. *Black Religion and American Evangelicalism: White Protestants, Plantation Missions, and the Flowering of Negro Christianity, 1787–1865*. Metuchen, N.J.: Scarecrow, 1975.

Sewall, Samuel. *The Selling of Joseph: A Memorial*. Edited by Sidney Kaplan. Amherst: University of Massachusetts Press, 1969.

Shields, John C. "Phillis Wheatley's Struggle for Freedom in Her Poetry and Prose." In *The Collected Works of Phillis Wheatley*, edited by Shields, 229–70. New York: Oxford University Press, 1988.

———. "Phillis Wheatley's Use of Classicism." *American Literature* 52, no. 1 (1980): 97–111.

Shuffelton, Frank, ed. *A Mixed Race: Ethnicity in Early America*. New York: Oxford University Press, 1993.

Simpson, Alan. *Puritanism in Old and New England*. Chicago: University of Chicago Press, 1955.

Smith, Eleanor. "Phillis Wheatley: A Black Perspective." *Journal of Negro Education* 43, no. 3 (1974): 401–7.

Stewart, Maria W. *Maria W. Stewart, America's First Black Woman Political Writer: Essays and Speeches*. Edited by Marilyn Richardson. Bloomington: Indiana University Press, 1987.

———. "Mrs. Stewart's Farewell Address to Her Friends in the City of Boston." In *Maria W. Stewart, America's First Black Woman Political Writer: Essays and Speeches*, edited by Marilyn Richardson, 65–74. Bloomington: Indiana University Press, 1987.

———. "Religion and the Pure Principles of Morality, the Sure Foundation on Which We Must Build." In *Maria W. Stewart, America's First Black Woman Political Writer: Essays and Speeches*, edited by Marilyn Richardson, 28–42. Bloomington: Indiana University Press, 1987.

Thornton, John Kelly. *Africa and Africans in the Making of the Atlantic World, 1400–1680*. New York: Cambridge University Press, 1992.

———. *Africa and Africans in the Making of the Atlantic World, 1400–1800*. 2nd ed. Cambridge: Cambridge University Press, 1998.

Twagilimana, Aimable. *Race and Gender in the Making of an African American Literary Tradition*. New York: Garland, 1997.

Walker, David. *David Walker's Appeal to the Coloured Citizens of the World*. Edited by Peter P. Hinks. University Park: Pennsylvania State University Press, 2000.

Walker, James W. St. G. *The Black Loyalists: The Search for a Promised Land in Nova Scotia and Sierra Leone, 1783–1870*. New York: Africana, 1976.

Walkes, Joseph A., Jr. *Black Square and Compass: Two Hundred Years of Prince Hall Freemasonry.* Richmond, Va.: Macoy Publishing and Masonic Supply, 1979.

Weinstein, Allen, Frank Otto Gatell, and David Sarasohn, eds. *American Negro Slavery: A Modern Reader.* 3rd ed. New York: Oxford University Press, 1979.

Wesley, Charles H. *Prince Hall: Life and Legacy.* 2nd ed. Washington, D.C.: United Supreme Council, Southern Jurisdiction, Prince Hall Affiliation, 1983.

Wheatley, Phillis. *The Collected Works of Phillis Wheatley.* Edited by John C. Shields. New York: Oxford University Press, 1988.

——. *Complete Writings.* Edited by Vincent Carretta. New York: Penguin, 2001.

Whitchurch, S. *The Negro Convert, a Poem, Being the Substance of the Experience of Mr. John Marrant, a Negro, as Related by Himself, Previous to His Ordination, at the Countess of Huntingdon's Chapel, in Bath, on Sunday the 15th of May, 1785, Together with a Concise Account of the Most Remarkable Events in His Very Singular Life.* Bath: Hazard, 1785.

White, Newman Ivey. *American Negro Folk-Songs.* Hatboro, Pa.: Folklore Associates, 1965.

Winiarski, Douglas L. "Souls Filled with Ravishing Transport: Heavenly Visions and the Radical Awakening in New England." *William and Mary Quarterly,* 3rd ser., 61, no. 1 (2004): 3–46.

Wood, Peter H. " 'Jesus Christ Has Got Thee at Last': Afro-American Conversion as a Forgotten Chapter in Eighteenth Century Intellectual History." *Bulletin for the Center for the Study of Southern Culture and Religion* 3, no. 3 (1979): 2–7.

Woodson, Carter G. *The History of the Negro Church.* 2nd ed. Washington, D.C.: Associated Publishers, 1945.

——. *The History of the Negro Church.* 3rd ed. Washington, D.C.: Associated Publishers, 1972.

INDEX

Abbot, Benjamin, 107
abolitionists: and black self-
determination, 122; and gradualism,
45; and Haitian Revolution, 87;
and Hammon, 48; immediatists
among, 9; and racism, 88–89;
and St. Paul, 36–37; mentioned,
135n17
accommodation, 41, 48, 60, 62, 91
Act of Toleration, 18
Adams, John, 101–2
African Lodge 459: as black institution,
97; Hall's charges to, 85, 92; Marrant
as chaplain of, 70, 82, 90; Marrant's
sermon to, 66, 78, 83
African Methodist Episcopal Church, 98,
101, 103–4, 106, 114
African Methodist Episcopal Zion
Church, 88
afterlife: and Christian beliefs, 26, 37–38;
contemplation of, 2, 24, 43, 56
Aldridge, William, 64, 80
Allen, Richard, 6, 94, 97, 98–115, 120,
138n18
American Revolution: black revolutionaries in, 7, 90; and Hammon, 1, 26, 33,
40–41, 62; and institution building,
83; and Marrant, 64, 65, 70, 82; and
theology, 57, 60; and Wheatley, 1,
50–51, 55, 62; white revolutionaries in,
7, 61, 63, 100
Andrews, William L., 88
antislavery: and biblical exegesis, 124,
131n43; and black self-determination,
89; and black writers, 24, 88; and
Haitian Revolution, 87; and Hammon,
42; and Marrant, 72, 74–75, 135n33; and
revolutionary ministers, 61

Appeal to the Coloured Citizens of the
World (Walker), 9, 105
Aptheker, Herbert, 93
Archbishop of Canterbury, 67
Arminianism, 30–31, 63, 65, 74, 81, 86
Asbury, Francis, 101, 107, 113
Ashworth, John, 26
authority: in Baptist Church, 22; biblical,
65, 90; civil, 34, 102; and class, 19; clergy
as, 25; and Countess of Huntingdon,
81; ecclesiastic, 13–15, 73, 79, 100, 108,
114; and Hammon, 40; and Marrant,
65; and Moravians, 67; and race, 85–88,
110–11

Baptist, 5, 12, 21–22
Bassard, Katherine Clay, 51, 61, 127n13,
132n6
Benezet, Anthony, 94
Bethel African Church, 101, 105, 110, 113–14
Bethesda Plantation, 74–75
Bible: as antislavery, 14, 26; and authority,
54, 65, 90, 93, 119; exegesis of, 78, 124;
literalism, 37; slave reactions to, 13, 46;
as support for slavery, 14, 36, 40
biblical typology, 50, 122
Birth of Tragedy, The (Nietzsche), 17
Black Arts movement, 50, 132n6
black church: development of, 17, 94,
98–101, 107, 128n24; difficulties
establishing, 113; and enthusiasm 20;
Philadelphia's first, 111; success of, 3–4,
127n8
black intellectualism, 9, 22–23
Black Power movement, 50, 132n6
Boston Evening Post, 49
broadsides, 1, 46
Bustill, Cyrus, 114

Cannon, William Ragsdale, 99
Carey, Matthew, 109
Carretta, Vincent, 7
chattel, 3, 13, 14, 29, 32, 40
Chauncy, Charles, 61
Chew, Benjamin, 106
Clarkson, Matthew, 109
Coke, Thomas, 107; *Journal of the Rev. Dr. Coke's Visit to Jamaica*, 74
Coker, Daniel, 114
conversion: doctrine of, 69, 78; in Marrant's *Narrative*, 80, 117; and slaves, 4, 12–14, 21, 29, 40; and Stewart, 118, 123
Cook, Samuel, 61
Cooper, Samuel, 61, 63
Countess of Huntingdon. *See* Hastings, Selina
covenanted community, 65, 71, 122
Creel, Margaret, 15, 128n24
cultural heritage, 4

death: corporeal, 38–39, 43, 59–61, 74; spiritual, 110
denominations, 15–17, 21, 100
depravity, 27–28, 30, 42–43
Dickins, John, 113
dissenters, 20, 67–68, 71, 129n10
double consciousness, 40
Douglass, Frederick, 88–89
Du Bois, W. E. B., 40, 127n8

Eagleton, Terry, 103
Easton, Hosea, 95
economics: and black exploitation, 87, 94; of black institution building, 83, 86; of slavery, 3, 5, 7, 13–15, 27, 37; of women's institution building, 123
Edwards, Jonathan, 65, 117, 133n24, 134n29; and Edwardian Calvinism, 44
elect, the, 29–31, 48
Enlightenment, the, 51–52, 54, 84–87, 99, 103

enthusiasm: as political expression, 13, 20, 22, 67; as spiritual sign, 4, 21; as tradition, 17–20
Episcopal Church of America, 101, 107, 113
epyllion, 52
Equiano, Olaudah, 68, 76
essentialism, 8
Ethiopia, 85, 87, 95
evangelicalism: and community building, 81, 105; and science, 52–54; and tradition, 77

faith: and the afterlife, 43; and Moravians, 18; outward expressions of, 4, 22; and predestination, 66; and science, 54; and spiritual crisis, 69, 106; and spreading the Gospel, 73; and works, 105, 125
Felder, Cain Hope, 122
Festival of St. John the Baptist, 78, 90–91, 94
folk traditions, 42, 46–47, 78, 85, 131n68
Franklin, Benjamin, 51, 111
Free African Society of Philadelphia, 94, 101, 108–12
Frey, Silvia R., 12
Fugitive Slave Law, 36, 102

Garrison, Freeborn, 106–7
Garrison, William Lloyd, 88–89, 106
gender, 116, 118–19, 123, 125, 139n1
George III, 58, 61
Gibson, Edmund, 14, 18–19, 28, 73, 130n16
Gorton, Samuel, 25
Gospel, the: and Allen, 103; effects of, on slaves, 13–14, 28; and Hammond, 26, 29, 34; and Marrant, 72–74, 77, 90; slave resistance to, 11; as social control, 21; and Stewart, 124; and Wheatley, 54
Gradual Emancipation Act, 34
gradualism, 41, 45, 76, 87
Gray, William, 108

Great Awakening, the: and Arminianism, 65; and Hammon, 33; and leadership, 15; and Marrant, 70; and slaves, 11, 13–14; spread of, 19, 21
Gullah people, 11

Haitian Revolution, 85, 87–88, 92, 95
Hall, Prince, 83–97, 103, 122
Hammon, Jupiter, 25, 48
Hastings, Selina, 51, 61, 66–71, 74–77, 80–81, 135n33
Hebrew, 29, 37, 57, 71, 139–40n4
Hegel, G. W. F., 9
Hinks, Peter P., 95
Hobbes, Thomas, 103
Hopkins, Samuel, 44, 60–61
Huntingdon Connection, 66, 75–76, 79–80
hush-harbor, 76

ideology: and Hammon, 42, 60; and institution building, 6, 84, 86; and literature, 88
Isani, Mukhtar Ali, 50
Israel, 29, 57, 104–5, 107, 120–22
itinerant ministry: and Allen, 99, 104, 107–8, 114; and the Great Awakening, 19; and Marrant, 64, 70; and Methodism, 21; and religious authority, 15

Jefferson, Thomas, 8, 50–51
John, Beverly M., 11
John Street Church, 88
Jones, Absalom, 94, 97, 101–2, 108–9, 112–14
Journal of the Rev. Dr. Coke's Visit to Jamaica (Coke), 74

Kant, Immanuel, 84–85
Kingdom of God. *See* Kingdom of Heaven
Kingdom of Heaven, 2, 38, 48, 61

Lapsansky, Philip, 90
Levernier, James A., 50
literacy: and African Americans, 11, 22, 33, 45, 84; and social status, 3, 86
Lloyd, Henry, 32
Lloyd, James, 32
Lloyd, Joseph, 26, 32
London Packet, 49
lord bishop of London. *See* Gibson, Edmund
loyalist, 26, 64–65, 70, 82–83, 86

Magaw, Samuel, 110–13
manumission, 33, 62–63
Margate, David, 74–76, 81, 104, 120
Marrant, John: as a Briton, 7; and Prince Hall Masons, 84, 91–92; as prophetic figure, 104, 120, 125; 1789 sermon, 88, 90; mentioned, 23, 63, 104, 117. *See also Narrative of the Lord's Wonderful Dealings with John Marrant, A*
Marsden, John, 67
master-slave relationship, 12, 26–27, 39, 40, 129n6
Mather, Cotton, 73; *The Negro Christianized*, 13–14
Methodism: African, 101, 103, 104, 110, 113; attacks on, 18–19; doctrines of, 18, 21, 66, 81–82; and emotionalism, 21; Huntingdonian, 67, 72, 79; organization of, 22, 107
Middle Passage, 2, 4
Modern Egyptians, 2, 122
Moravians, 18, 67

Narrative of the Lord's Wonderful Dealings with John Marrant, A (Marrant): amanuensis of, 78; and Christian theology, 71, 79–81; and Countess of Huntingdon, 75–76; and Jenkins Plantation, 66, 72, 76; popularity of, 8, 65–66, 70; and slavery, 69, 72, 74–75

Negro Christianized, The (Mather), 13–14
Negro Convert, The (Whitchurch), 80
New Divinity, 44
New Light Calvinism, 70–71, 78
Newman, Richard, 90
Newton, Isaac, 52, 133n21
Nicholson, John, 108
Nietzsche, Friedrich, 17
Northwest Ordinance, 93
Notes on the State of Virginia (Jefferson), 8, 51

Occom, Samson, 55, 61
Old Light Calvinism, 33
Old South Meeting House, 61
O'Neale, Sondra, 50, 128n1
Onesimus, 36–37, 39–40
orality, 17, 46–48, 77, 85, 96
ordination sermon, 64–67, 69–72, 75, 80

paganism, 28–29, 96, 110–11
Paine, Thomas, 84–85, 92
Pantheon, 67
paternalism, 27, 32, 41–42, 75–76, 110–11
Patterson, Orlando, 7, 10, 12, 48
Paul, St.: Hammon's understanding of, 26–27, 35, 38, 42; and irresistible grace, 65; Marrant's understanding of, 90; and master-slave relationship, 39, 129n6, 129n8; support of, for slavery, 13–14, 36–38, 73; and suspicion of enthusiasm, 19; and women, 124–25
Pauline Mandate, 36
Pemberton, Ebenezer, 61
Pennsylvania Society for the Abolition of Slavery, 111
perpetual servitude, 10, 12, 41, 60
perseverance of the saints, 30–31
Peters, Erskine, 40, 131n57
petitions, 33–34, 89, 102, 123, 136n2
Phaedrus, 17
Philadelphia African School, 94
Philemon, 36, 39–40

Phillips Academy, 107
Philosophy of History, The (Hegel), 9
piety, 21, 28, 54–55, 83
planters, 13, 73
Plato, 17
Poems on Various Subjects (Wheatley), 1, 8, 50, 52–57, 59, 61
predestination: and covenanted communities, 66; and Huntingdonian Methodism, 64–65, 80; and nationalism, 57; and sainthood, 31; and slavery, 25; and works, 63
proof-texting, 50
public education, 83, 91, 94
Puritan, 2, 66, 69, 70

Quakers, 34, 94, 100

Raboteau, Albert, 47, 98, 127n2
racism, 4, 16, 88, 98, 116
Rael, Patrick, 90
rationality: and the Enlightenment, 99; fear as, 30; and literacy, 86, 96; and religion, 28; and resistance, 84–85; regeneration, 30, 38; and the unregenerated, 28–30
repentance, 27, 38, 69
revivalism, 12, 65
Revolutionary War, 40–41, 64, 90, 107
Robinson, William H., 50
Rush, Benjamin, 51, 100, 108–9, 112

Saint George's Methodist Church, 98–101, 108, 113–14
Saint Thomas's African Protestant Episcopal Church, 100–101, 112–14
Scheick, William J., 8
Selling of Joseph, The (Sewell), 14
sermons: extemporaneous, 77; of Hammon, 25; of Marrant, 75, 78; as resistance, 87, 89
Sewell, Samuel, 16, 61; *The Selling of Joseph*, 14

Sharp, Granville, 51, 61, 100
Shays' Rebellion, 91–92
Shields, John, 50
Sierra Leone, 64, 67
sin: and the individual, 69, 117–18; as justified by God, 24, 35, 42–44; and saints, 31; and slavery, 57–58, 104; slaves' concept of, 11–12; and society, 26, 28, 121
slave codes, 9, 15, 88
Spa Fields Chapel, 67–68, 81
Stamp Act, 1, 58
Stewart, Maria W.: as prophet, 117; and women's evangelicalism, 117–25, 139n1, 139n4, 140n9, 140n16; mentioned, 63, 97, 114
Sturgis, Stokeley, 102

Tabernacle Chapel, 61, 81
Terrence, 62
Thornton, John, 61, 90–91, 93
tokenism, 6, 8
Trevecca College, 67–69, 77–78

Unitas Fratrum (Moravians), 18, 67
universal republicanism, 2, 71
U.S. Constitution, 90, 93

vernacular, 51, 77–78, 132n6
Virginia Gazette, 51

Walker, David, 97, 108, 114, 122; *Appeal to the Coloured Citizens of the World*, 9, 105
Washington, George, 51, 62–63
Wegelin, Oscar, 45
Wesley, John: and *Arminian Magazine*, 63; and first Methodist General Conference, 107; and the Great Awakening, 19, 21; and Marrant, 78, 81; Moravian influence on, 18; on slavery, 75–76; and Wesleyan Methodism, 64, 74
Whatcoat, Richard, 107
Wheatley, Phillis: as evangelical writer, 50, 56, 133n22; *Poems on Various Subjects*, 1, 8, 50, 52–57, 59, 61; political poetry of, 57, 60; on slavery, 1–2
Whitchurch, Samuel, 64, 68–69; *The Negro Convert*, 80
Whitefield, George, 21, 61, 65, 68, 75, 81
Williams, Peter, 87–88
Williams, Roger, 25
Wood, Betty, 12
Wood, Peter H., 70
Woolridge, Thomas, 61

yellow fever, 6, 106, 108–11